Αφιερωμένο στην γιαγιά μου Ασημίνα,
συνονόματή και δασκάλα
μου στο μαγείρεμα

Dedicated to my yiayia, Asimina,
my namesake and cooking teacher

ISBN: 978-0-9847210-7-8
Printed in China through Asia Pacific Offset
Third printing, 2022

COOKING FOR ARTISTS

Well, Art is Art, isn't it? Still, on the other hand, water is water. And east is east and west is west and if you take cranberries and stew them like applesauce they taste much more like prunes than rhubarb does. Now you tell me what you know.

—*Groucho Marx,* Animal Crackers

Cassandra MacLeod, *Purrr-a Vida*, 2014

WHY ANOTHER COOKBOOK?

Five years ago Mina cooked for a large party at the studio. Since then we never let her go.

We ate so much good food here; we were continually surprised; we became educated and at times spoiled. As one might imagine, cooking for the same people every day is not an easy task; however, Mina took the challenge in stride. Over the years, her repertoire kept expanding, as she was never afraid to experiment and grow. Every morning when Mina walked through the door, grocery bags in hand, she was greeted with a big *YAY!* In the process of feeding us, she came up with many new dishes, trying new variations, all the while progressing self-critically with confidence. We learned so much from her generosity—most of all, that fear does not belong in cooking. We came to understand that the main ingredient in cooking is love.

As we believe that good things should be shared to enrich our lives, the idea of this cookbook came about. A lot of the recipes in this book are a reflection of this wonderful time.

We are in the midst of a much-needed food renaissance. For generations, most of us grew up with processed and industrialized food. A lot of our culinary heritage has gotten lost as parts of our identity became commodified. The more digital our lives become, the more we feel the urge to emulate a wholesome past we never had. Imagine a Norman Rockwell painting of people in a farm-to-table restaurant on their smartphones. Food has always been one of the foundations of our identities, whether we find it in fashionable diets, organic ingredients, or our mothers' cooking.

Organic foods should not have to be labeled "organic." What should be labeled is everything else. There is a lot of information out there about what types of food are good for you or what not to eat. Many recent culinary movements bring something new to the table and there are great ideas to be learned from the more radical approaches of the last decades. Mina Stone's cooking embraces many of them, without getting caught up in any of their dogmas. You could say her cooking is post-dogmatic.

We hope the future feels a little like that.

Mina first shared her personal approach to cooking through posting recipes and photographs of her creations on her blog. It was real food that was cooked to be eaten. This is the spirit we maintained for the format of this book—all images taken by Mina of real meals she cooked that we happily ate.

Informed by many lessons learned from her grandmother in Greece, Mina's food is a direct reflection of a simple approach to feeding your family with what is readily available in the local market, the garden, or in nature. Funnily enough, that makes for a very healthy meal. Her recipes are very straightforward. Fish is fish, meat is meat, and vegetables are vegetables. For those of us who don't eat animals, this makes it very easy.

When Mina is in the kitchen, you can catch her standing by the stove, tasting and chewing slowly. It looks like she is in another world, where food comes alive in her mind. One can only imagine how it must be to think in flavors, not words or images. We often wonder how it's possible as she continues cooking, preparing dish after dish with such grace and great calm. One secret we have learned while observing her is that some courses can be served at room temperature and not everything needs to be piping hot. This makes room for the cook to enjoy the process. The resulting lunch is comprised of several beautiful, balanced dishes that effortlessly marry color, texture, flavor, and nutrition.

It looks like food will always absorb the cook's demeanor.

—Urs, Alex, and PR

COOKING FOR ARTISTS

A text exchange:

Me: *Corinna, hi! Remember the very first dinner I cooked at GBE? Forty people, chicken bouillabaisse and rice? Who was that for? And what was the theme? I'm forgetting so much, I should have kept track of everything better...* 😬

Corinna: *It might have been Peter Doig? Does that sound familiar? It was inspired by something I had read about the 19th-century French art dealer Ambroise Vollard. He hosted dinners in his cellar and made chicken curry—which you would not agree to. Your compromise was the bouillabaisse.*
I think I had seen the Vollard show at the Met around that time. I can find the picture of the painting we used for the invite—one of Vollard's famous dinners. It seemed so chic in the best way—a Russian aristocrat collector sitting next to an artist eating a simple meal cooked by Vollard himself. Supposedly it was a very sought-after invitation...

So, that was the beginning.

Sometime in winter, 2006. We still haven't been able to figure out when the opening was, exactly.

I was twenty-four years old and had no idea what I was getting into.

I was freshly out of art school with a BFA in fashion and my own small line of dresses. I started cooking to support myself while I tried to build my label, and—long story short—I realized I crawled into bed with cookbooks much more often than with *Vogue*.

I was never formally trained. I learned mostly on my own, mostly from cooking shows (*yes!*), and mostly from my eighty-six-year-old Greek yiayia, who cooks every single day the most delicious food you've ever had. She taught me to boil potatoes before roasting them, to make them extra-crispy and soft. She taught me to add the bulk of the olive oil after the food was cooked for full flavor and health. She taught me how to make chickpeas meltingly tender and transform them into the best stew with only four ingredients. She taught me how to cook in order to please people—figuring out what they like and incorporating it into the dish at hand, making more than you need, and going the extra mile.

I have the grandma who cooks better than anyone else you know and shows her love through cooking. I've gotten to pick Yiayia's olives and harvest the purest olive oil. Bright green and smooth, it's always stored in big red plastic containers kept in the basement that occasionally floods. I get to escort her to the *laiki* (farmer's market), which is so very different from American ones. The Greek farmer's market is more like the stock exchange—there's lots of hollering and waving of different fruits and vegetables for the best bargain and highest quality. I've been lucky to have these experiences with her and even luckier to be able to cook professionally for the people I cook for.

I titled this book *Cooking for Artists* simply because it is what I have been doing for the past nine years. I realized I had something to say about what that experience has been like for me: I don't think I could have ever developed my own style of cooking so naturally under any other circumstances. From the very first menu for a gallery dinner at Gavin Brown's enterprise in 2006 to years of lunches at the studio of Urs Fischer, I have always enjoyed the privilege of cooking essentially whatever I want.

My food is inspired by Greece, by different colors and textures, by people and experiences. Food should be balanced, the components of a menu working in harmony together from starters to dessert. Food should be beautiful, and should make you feel healthy and happy when the meal is done.

That is how I cook, but I don't have a strict philosophy for cooking other than to not have a strict philosophy.

I like going to farmer's markets, because yes, they have superior produce and beautiful salad greens.

They also have those little donuts covered in cinnamon and sugar.

I like going to the supermarket around the corner from my house because they have Mexican chilis I can't find anywhere else, and packages of chicken feet.

I like going to the Greek supermarket because I could buy a vacuum and a bathing suit along with my bright red tomatoes.

I like organic, local produce and I buy it a lot, but not always. I don't use bouillon, store-bought stocks, or seasoning blends.

I do, however, use good extra-virgin olive oil, *always*, and in quantity.

You know how in most cookbooks they have that fun section after the intro, suggesting what to keep in your pantry and explaining certain ingredients and different techniques and all that good stuff? My section is shorter. It's one concept and three main ingredients.

Here is the concept: Learn how to season. The best food this planet has to offer is best prepared simply, and simple food requires good seasoning. And guess what? It is not hard to do.

The main three ingredients I use to season are olive oil, lemon juice, and salt. My own personal holy trinity.

Extra-Virgin Olive Oil:
I consider olive oil to be a main ingredient in a lot of my recipes. I use more than most people, and good-quality olive oil makes all the difference. Olive oil can transform a boiled vegetable into the most luxurious and delicious item on your menu. It can elevate a simple vegetable soup to one with a rich consistency that's better than cream or butter. Avoid the mixed, cheaper brands of olive oil from who-knows-where. Try to buy cold-pressed extra-virgin olive oil from a single variety of olive, or a blend of olives that are all from the same region. The best thing to do is buy a 34-ounce tin from a Greek or Middle Eastern specialty store where the prices are low and the olive oil is exceptional.

Lemon Juice:
Bright and tangy, lemon juice is found in a lot of Greek cooking and in almost all of my recipes. From simply boiled greens and salad dressings to soups, fish, and braises, and as a condiment for grilled meats, lemon juice is always present. Note that when you add lemon juice (or any acid) to something, it cuts the salt and you then need to add a bit more than you might have otherwise.

Salt:
Unsalted food is sad food. It's food that never got to realize its full potential because it didn't have to chance to develop its flavor. When you can't figure out what is missing, or there is a flatness to something you make, the culprit is usually salt. So, experiment. If you are unsure what is ailing your dish, remove a spoonful and sprinkle it with a little salt. See if it becomes more pleasing to taste.

When following the recipes in this cookbook, you will find that I generally do not specify what kind of salt to use (kosher, sea salt, etc.). Use what you have on hand, armed with this information: Kosher salt is easy to sprinkle and it is less salty than sea salt and table salt, giving you more control over the seasoning. I like to use kosher salt in soups. It is also great for seasoning meats and fish because of its bigger grains, which help create a nice crust with less "saltiness." I like to use fine-grain sea salt for nuts, salads, and roasted potatoes, as it adheres to the food better and the finer grain is more appropriate. If I don't have kosher salt on hand, I use sea salt; if I don't have sea salt on hand, I use kosher salt.

When people ask me what kind of food I make, I always respond with "simple food." When people ask me what is in a dish, I usually respond with "olive oil, lemon juice, and salt."

I structured this cookbook to reflect my cooking style as closely as possible—which is to say that if I don't have one ingredient on hand, there are many others that work just as well. It is a style celebrating the inherent quality of flexibility that cooking encompasses—it's easy to play around with ingredients, and unless you are cooking an intricate recipe (you won't find any in this book), measurements never have to be exact. My approach to cooking is to have everything be as easy and stress-free as possible.

I hope these recipes inspire you, the same way I was inspired cooking for a bunch of crazy-in-the-best-way-possible creative people who allowed the kitchen to be my studio where I could do whatever I wanted . . . as long as it was tasty.

—Mina Stone

Lunch with Yiayia, Aegina, Greece

Temple of Aphaia, Aegina, Greece

FAMILY STYLE

It is a truism that food brings people together, that it is the social glue that binds us. But I believe this truism as a powerful fact that should not be overlooked—a fact that Mina Stone has, in the past nine years, made evident to me and to the countless other people she has fed at the gallery.

The idea of a cookbook of Mina's food brings, for me at least, conflicting emotions to the surface. I think I must have eaten everything here, and that is a strange thought when it comes to a book of recipes. Poring over these pages provides me with the exquisite opportunity to bask in the memory of the transitory delights of dinners gone by. This book feels less like a voyage through the unfamiliar than a chance to go back and relive some of the best and happiest meals I have ever had.

Post-opening gallery dinners are not a social convention; they are a vital part of the celebration of art and an artist's work. The notion of "breaking bread" (so apt in this context because her meals are always served "family-style"—an expression I had never heard before Mina started feeding us) is a simple but extraordinarily rich metaphor, and the act is as ancient and as fundamental to our nature as art itself. They are inseparable. How else should we celebrate the best of ourselves?

But, unlike Vollard, I don't cook. To invite people to eat with you and not serve something delicious seems like bad manners, so it has been the luck of a lifetime that Mina stepped into the breach every time. Every time she serves something delicious. There is nothing pretentious about her food—its purpose is to caress and satisfy. She does not show off or wear a struggle on her sleeve. She works in the spirit of the inspired, enthusiastic amateur—the same spirit as the artist's—and like the best art, her food has a deceptive straightforwardness, an honest clarity that tastes like the truth. It tastes yummy.

The recipes and photos in this book conjure the faces of happy, satisfied friends, nodding in agreement at the undeniable purity of her food and the joy of dining together. They remind me what a pleasure it is to feed people and of how many times Mina has done that on my behalf. That the gallery is in any way known as a place that values food and the sharing of food is almost entirely due to her efforts.

—*Gavin Brown*

Moni Island, Greece

Cooking gallery dinners for hundreds of hungry people, I've learned a few tricks for keeping everyone (myself included) happy and content. There is something special about walking into a room and encountering a table already set with beautiful platters of starters to nibble on. Bountiful snacks or mezze encourage a relaxed environment, tiding over hungry guests as they talk and sample the treats laid out before them, while keeping the cook stress-free to finish making the meal.

Starters should feel like a warm welcome to the dinner table, a sneak peek of what's to come. The best starters are those that can be made ahead of time, or involve very little preparation. For every dinner I like to fill the tables with bowls of tangy vegetables and fresh herbs, and cutting boards laden with cured meats and cheeses. Sometimes I throw in a mezze or two if I am feeling super-fancy. Try to make your platters look beautiful, and balanced in colors and textures. If you see an unusual vegetable at the market that pops with color, like a bright watermelon radish or a pretty purple carrot, throw that into the mix as well.

STARTERS

VEGETABLES WITH LEMON JUICE AND SALT

This is my favorite trick for raw vegetables. All you have to do is squeeze lots of lemon juice and sprinkle salt on them and people think you have performed some sort of miracle. Extra lemon juice, extra salt. That's the key. I don't specify quantities because you can cut up as many or as few vegetables as you want, depending on how many people you're having over. The idea is to squeeze enough lemon juice over the vegetables so that they are super-tangy.

cucumbers, radishes, or carrots
fresh lemon juice
salt
fresh mint leaves, flat-leaf parsley leaves, and/or thinly sliced jalapeños (optional)

Wash and trim the vegetables and cut them in a way that looks pretty—carrots on the bias, radishes in half-moons, or cucumbers with a bit of green peel on each slice.

Squeeze lots of lemon over the sliced vegetables and sprinkle generously with salt.

You can add fresh herbs or thinly sliced jalapeños as a garnish, depending on what you have on hand.

Serve with cheese, bread, and olives, or as a side to the Whipped Feta (page 20) or Beet Tzatziki (page 25).

KOPANISTI (WHIPPED FETA)

Deliciousness occurs when you mix salty feta with creamy ricotta and spicy red pepper flakes. This is great as a dip for vegetables or bread, and is also a welcome addition to any sandwich.

Serves 6–8

¾ cup Greek or French feta
½ cup whole-milk ricotta
½ teaspoon hot red pepper flakes (add more to make it spicier)
a pinch of dried oregano
⅓ cup extra-virgin olive oil, plus more for drizzling

In a food processor, pulse the feta, ricotta, hot red pepper flakes, and oregano together while pouring the olive oil through the feed tube. It should take about one minute to come together; you are looking for a smooth and creamy consistency similar to peanut butter. Add more olive oil as necessary.

Transfer the mixture to a serving dish and drizzle with more olive oil if desired. Serve with grilled bread, vegetables, and olives.

ELIES TSAKISTES (OLIVES WITH CORIANDER SEEDS AND LEMON PEEL)

This is a bastardized version of some amazing olives I had on a trip to Cyprus. The Cypriots have their own distinct Greek dialect and I could barely understand what anyone said the entire time I was there, but I wasn't leaving until I understood how they make their olives so fragrant and delicious.

My friend's mother told me that the Cypriots marinate them in garlic, lemon peel, and whole coriander seeds that have been toasted and then crushed with the back of a spoon. In this version, regular green olives are quick-marinated in the same mixture with the addition of a few rosemary leaves for tasty and aromatic results.

Makes 1 cup olives

2 tablespoons whole coriander seeds
1 cup Castelvetrano or Picholine olives
1 garlic clove, peeled and sliced in thirds (optional)
2 slices of lemon peel
a few fresh rosemary leaves
extra-virgin olive oil

In a dry pan over low heat, toast the coriander seeds until they are fragrant. Some of them might actually pop as popcorn does.

Crush the toasted seeds with the back of a spoon in the pan. Remove from the pan and toss them in a bowl with the olives, garlic (if using), lemon peel, and rosemary leaves. Add a drizzle of olive oil to allow everything to marinate.

BEET TZATZIKI WITH WALNUTS AND MINT

With its vibrantly pink color and flecks of bright green mint, this dish is not only beautiful, but a wonderfully different take on traditional cucumber tzatziki. The grated raw beets hold up well against the yogurt, and their sweetness is balanced by the toasted walnuts and fresh mint. Beet tzatziki is delicious served with fresh bread or alongside braised meat, roasted potatoes, vegetables, or lentils.

Serves 6–8

2 medium red beets
2 cups whole-milk Greek yogurt
1 or 2 garlic cloves (depending on your preference), finely minced
½ cup raw walnuts, toasted using Technique #1 (page 34) and finely chopped
2 tablespoons fresh lemon juice
3 tablespoons extra-virgin olive oil
1 handful of fresh mint leaves, finely chopped; reserve a pinch for garnish
salt and freshly ground black pepper

Peel the beets with a vegetable peeler or small knife and grate them on the coarse side of a grater. Drain the grated beets by pressing them in a colander, or wrapping them in cheesecloth or paper towels to absorb the excess moisture. Add the beets to the yogurt and stir. Add the minced garlic to the beet/yogurt mixture. I use a single clove of garlic for a milder tzatziki and two for a strong garlic flavor.

Stir the walnuts, lemon juice, olive oil, chopped mint, a pinch of salt, and a grinding of black pepper into the yogurt mixture. Taste the tzatziki for seasoning, adding more lemon juice and salt if necessary. Garnish with the remaining chopped mint leaves.

TARTINES WITH PARMESAN, HONEY, AND THYME

This was on the very first menu I cooked at GBE back in 2006 and it was a runaway hit. A tartine is a very sweet little French way to describe a piece of bread spread with butter, honey, jam, cheese, and the like, and this is just that. I like using olive oil and I like using butter as well. They both combine with honey in that oozy delicious way with the addition of savory Parmesan and fresh thyme. It is as if a Greek got lost . . . zipping through Provence on a Vespa.

Serves 8–10

1 baguette, sliced into ¼-inch diagonal pieces
extra-virgin olive oil or unsalted butter
½ cup Parmesan cheese, thinly sliced with a mandoline or vegetable peeler
honey
1 heaping tablespoon fresh thyme leaves
freshly ground black pepper

Preheat the oven to 400 °F.

Drizzle the sliced baguette with olive oil, or spread a little butter onto every slice. Toast on a baking sheet in the oven for about 5 minutes, just until the bread is light golden brown. Remove bread from the oven.

Drizzle each piece of bread with honey and arrange two or three slices of Parmesan on top. Finish with another drizzle of honey and then sprinkle with fresh thyme leaves and ground black pepper. Serve immediately.

Beans
SALT
Olive
Oil

This page: Gavin Brown's enterprise, New York

Opposite page: Josh Smith, 2015

I make most of my salads with two concepts in mind. One: keep the salad super-simple, with lots of lemon juice, a drizzle of good olive oil, salt, and freshly ground black pepper. Two: incorporate a different dimension such as the richness of Parmesan cheese, the savory crunchiness of a toasted nut, the freshness of an unexpected herb, or all three. Heartier cruciferous vegetables such as cabbage, cauliflower, and brussels sprouts work the best with toasted nuts and herbs because when thinly sliced, they stand up well to the weight of richer ingredients.

SALADS

Laiki Piraeus, Greece

SALAD DRESSINGS

When it comes to salad dressing, I make the same base every time, with little twists. I always start with lemon juice and extra-virgin olive oil. I use vinegar sparingly and on rare occasions. Lemon juice is usually my acid of choice for vegetables and greens, as it tastes bright, citrusy, and clean. When I make salad for a lot of people, I like to have my dressing already made and combined, and store whatever is left in the fridge.

I also dress salad directly in the bowl: first, with a light drizzle of olive oil, and then with a squeeze of lemon juice. I do it in this order so that the greens have a protective coating and don't wilt with the addition of the lemon juice. Always taste for seasoning before serving.

FRESH LEMON JUICE DRESSING

¼ cup fresh lemon juice
⅔ cup extra-virgin olive oil
salt and freshly ground black pepper
finely chopped shallots and/or a spoonful of good mustard (optional)

Whisk the olive oil into the lemon juice. Add salt and pepper to taste. If using shallots, let them sit in the lemon juice for 5 minutes before whisking in the olive oil. If using mustard, whisk into the lemon juice before whisking in the olive oil.

TANGY SOUR CREAM DRESSING

¼ cup fresh lemon juice
½ cup sour cream
¼ cup extra-virgin olive oil
salt and freshly ground black pepper

Whisk together the lemon juice and sour cream. Then whisk in the olive oil and add salt and pepper to taste.

GREEN GODDESS SPIN-OFF

Prepare the Tangy Sour Cream Dressing (feel free to substitute buttermilk for the sour cream or use a combination of both). Using a food processor, blend the dressing with a cup of all or one of the following fresh herbs: flat-leaf parsley, tarragon, mint, and cilantro leaves.

TAHINI DRESSING

This dressing is great with sturdy roasted vegetables such as Roasted Cauliflower (page 97) and lentil and rice dishes such as *Mujaddara* (page 128). It's also the dressing I use for Grated Beet, Carrot, Radish, and Avocado Salad (page 46).

scant ¼ cup fresh lemon juice
½ cup tahini
¼ cup extra-virgin olive oil
salt and freshly ground black pepper

Whisk the lemon juice into the tahini and then whisk in the olive oil, seasoning with salt and freshly ground black pepper.

NUTS AND SEEDS

Nuts and seeds are a crucial component to many of my recipes. I love the texture and (for lack of a better word) nuttiness they add to salads, pastas, and grains. My cousin Margarita came to visit me from Athens and when she opened my fridge was horrified to find "only nuts and seeds!" and nothing she could actually eat. Upon her return to Greece, she reported this to our relatives as a fun and cute little story, and, as with all good Greek families, it was turned into a proper family drama featuring my lack of food and manners when receiving a family member from abroad. Margarita is right, though; I have a lot of nuts and seeds in my refrigerator (which is the best place to store them so they stay fresh).

Using raw, high-quality nuts and seeds and toasting them yourself makes all the difference. I toast nuts two different ways depending on the quantity or what dish they're going into.

TECHNIQUE #1: DRY-TOASTING NUTS IN THE OVEN

This is a dry roast without any olive oil or salt. Use this method for larger nuts like whole almonds, walnuts, and hazelnuts, and to toast larger quantities. I never use this technique for pine nuts, as I find that the wet-toasting method (see Technique #2) works much better.

Set your rack in the center of the oven, and preheat the oven to 325 °F. Spread the nuts on a baking sheet and roast for 8 to 10 minutes. Check often until you see an even golden color. Remove from the oven and cool the nuts completely before adding them to your recipe.

TECHNIQUE #2: WET-TOASTING NUTS IN A PAN

I toast nuts and seeds in a pan when I want to coat them in a nice layer of olive oil and salt. I like to use this technique when I want the nuts to really stand out in a recipe. I only toast pine nuts this way—they come out with a much nicer golden sheen.

Place a frying pan over very low heat on the stove and add the nuts or seeds in an even layer so that they don't overlap too much. Add a drizzle of olive oil, just enough to evenly coat all the nuts, and a generous sprinkle of fine sea salt so there is a light "dust" on every nut. Sauté until the nuts are fragrant and golden brown, around 5 to 7 minutes. This takes time, so be patient, and remember to shake the pan often so the nuts toast evenly. Cool the nuts on a paper towel to absorb any excess oil before adding them to your recipe.

PRASINI SALATA (GREEN SALAD)

This is a staple wintertime salad in Greece, when romaine is in season. It is a very simple salad that is fresh and delicious. The trick to all salads, but most importantly the simple ones, is to make sure they're well-dressed. You need just enough olive oil to lightly coat the greens, and enough salt and lemon juice for the flavors to really pop. I have never seen a Greek person prepare a salad dressing in advance, so in this recipe the salad is dressed the old-fashioned way: in the bowl.

Serves 6–8

1 head of romaine lettuce, outer leaves removed
2 handfuls of fresh dill, chopped
3 scallions, finely chopped
extra-virgin olive oil
juice of 1 lemon
salt and freshly ground black pepper

Cut the base off the romaine and wash all the leaves, keeping them whole. Dry the leaves with a paper towel and stack them about 3 or 4 at a time. Cut the leaves cross-wise into ¼-inch ribbons. Place the romaine in a bowl and top with the chopped dill and scallions. Dress the salad by drizzling with olive oil and squeezing the lemon juice over it.

Sprinkle with salt and freshly ground black pepper, and toss the salad at the table when serving.

EARLY SPRING SALAD

This is a salad I get very excited to make after months of New York City winter hell. There are a few weeks in March where I just cannot stomach another squash or sweet potato. And then! Snap peas, asparagus, radishes—the whole lot comes all at once and makes the best salad of early spring produce. I love to dress this salad simply—with olive oil and lemon juice, in order to let the veggies shine. For a creamy and more indulgent salad, use Tangy Sour Cream Dressing (page 33).

Serves 6

6 generous cups of salad greens of your choice (red romaine leaves, red butter lettuce, arugula, baby chard, or baby kale leaves)
1 handful of fresh mint leaves, roughly torn
3–4 stalks of asparagus, cut as thinly as possible on the bias
2 handfuls of snap peas, cut on the bias
3–4 radishes, thinly sliced
½ cup good-quality Pecorino, shaved into ribbons with a vegetable peeler
Fresh Lemon Juice Dressing or Tangy Sour Cream Dressing (page 33)
salt and freshly ground black pepper

In a large bowl, place the salad greens and half of the mint, chopped asparagus, snap peas, radishes, and shaved Pecorino.

Prepare the dressing of your choice and toss.

Scatter the remaining vegetables and Pecorino on top of the salad. Finish with a sprinkle of salt and a grinding of black pepper.

HERB SALAD WITH FETA AND TOASTED ALMONDS

This is a slightly labor-intensive salad because who really wants to pick little leaves off of mint and parsley stems . . . ? But, hey, if you're in the mood, it is worth it and it's delicious. I've made this salad for eighty people. So there.

Serves 4

2 bunches of fresh flat-leaf parsley
1 bunch of fresh mint
1 bunch of fresh cilantro
1 small handful of fresh tarragon leaves
Fresh Lemon Juice Dressing (page 33)
½ cup raw sliced almonds, toasted using Technique #1 (page 34)
1 cup Greek or French feta, crumbled

Wash all of the herbs and dry with paper towels. Pick off the leaves, discard the stems, and place the leaves in a large bowl.

Toss the herbs with the dressing, using just enough for a light coating. Reserve the remaining dressing for another use.

Gently toss the herbs with the almonds and feta and serve.

HEIRLOOM TOMATOES WITH FETA AND MINT

This is one of those salads that needs lots of good bread—plain or toasted with garlic—to soak up the juicy tomatoes and salty feta.

If you can get your hands on it, use purslane in place of the micro greens. Purslane is an amazing little weed that grows all over Greece, New York, and many other places. You can get it at the farmer's market during the summer months, or potentially in your own backyard. It adds prettiness and texture to salads, and is an extremely healthy little plant chock full of omega-3s.

Serves 8

4 large heirloom tomatoes
extra-virgin olive oil
1 pound French or Greek feta, crumbled
1 small handful of fresh mint, chopped
1 cup micro greens or purslane, leaves only
¼ cup Kalamata or Picholine olives, pitted and coarsely chopped
salt and fresh ground black pepper

Slice the tomatoes into ¼-inch-thick circular discs, so you get about 4 or 5 discs from each tomato. Place the slices on a large platter in one layer and drizzle them with olive oil and a sprinkle of salt.

Top the tomato slices with crumbled feta, mint, chopped olives, and micro greens or purslane. Drizzle with olive oil once more, and finish with freshly ground pepper.

Variations:
Experiment with other fresh soft cheeses such as goat or farmer's cheese as a substitute for the feta.

GRATED BEET, CARROT, RADISH, AND AVOCADO SALAD WITH TAHINI DRESSING

There was a time when we decided to do vegan lunches for a month at the studio. I was okay at the beginning, but towards the end, I began to lose my cool a little bit. I started googling "best vegan food blogs" and found myself buying purified water, roasted dandelion tea, cashew milk, and raw cacao. I was reaching the point of no return, but when it comes down to it, freshly grated vegetables tossed in a thick and tangy tahini dressing are as tasty as they are healthy. It's nice to toss the grated carrots and radishes with the dressing in one bowl, and the beets in another. This way, you can carefully toss handfuls of the dressed beets into the carrots and keep the colors pretty and separate.

Serves 8–10

4 carrots, peeled and grated
1 daikon radish, peeled and grated
1 watermelon radish, grated (substitute a second daikon if you can't find a watermelon radish)
2 medium red beets, peeled and grated
Tahini Dressing (page 33)
fresh lemon juice
2 ripe avocados
salt and freshly ground black pepper

Place the grated carrots and radishes in one bowl and the grated beets in another.

Peel and slice the avocados thinly or into bite-size pieces and set aside.

Toss the carrots and radishes with some of the dressing, and toss the beets with the rest. Taste for seasoning and add more salt or lemon juice as needed. Before serving, combine the carrots and radishes with the beets. Top with the avocado and lots of freshly ground black pepper.

RAW CORN SALAD WITH TOASTED ALMONDS AND LIME

This salad has been described to me as something akin to Pop Rocks candy. The different textures and flavors burst in your mouth as you eat it. From the sweet corn kernels to the salty, crunchy almonds and aromatic herbs, it is a party of a salad.

Serves 4–6

5 ears of corn, shucked and washed
1 fresh jalapeño, finely chopped (optional)
2 large handfuls of flat-leaf parsley, chopped
½ cup whole raw almonds, toasted using Technique #1 (page 34) and coarsely chopped
extra-virgin olive oil
juice of 2 limes
salt and freshly ground black pepper

Run a sharp knife down the length of each ear of corn to separate the kernels from the cob. This is easiest done over a large bowl. Discard the cobs.

Toss the corn kernels with the jalapeño (if using) and parsley. Toss in the toasted almonds and then dress with a generous drizzle of olive oil and the juice of 2 limes. The salad should taste quite tangy. Sprinkle with salt and freshly ground black pepper to taste and serve.

Variations:
Add a handful of cherry tomatoes, sliced in half.
Add diced avocado, or different herbs, such as mint or cilantro. Anything works here with the corn base.

CABBAGE SALAD WITH APPLES, PUMPKIN SEEDS, AND AVOCADO

Lovely to look at and full of different textures and flavors, this salad is one that reminds me of California health foodies in the best way possible.

Serves 6–8

1 medium head of red or green cabbage, very thinly sliced
1 tart apple (such as Granny Smith or Pink Lady), diced
2 large handfuls of flat-leaf parsley, coarsely chopped
⅓ cup raw pumpkin seeds, toasted using Technique #2 (page 34)
1 avocado, sliced
Fresh Lemon Juice Dressing or Tangy Sour Cream Dressing (page 33)
1 handful of micro greens (pretty, but totally unnecessary if you don't have them)
salt and freshly ground black pepper

In a big bowl, mix the cabbage, apple, parsley, and toasted pumpkin seeds together.
Toss with the dressing of your choice. Add salt and pepper to taste.
Before serving, scatter avocado around the plate, and top with a handful of micro greens (if using).

SHAVED BRUSSELS SPROUTS WITH PARMESAN AND ALMONDS

This salad is the crème de la crème of the brussels sprout world. They held their annual conference and unanimously voted that Parmesan, toasted almonds, lemon, and olive oil are the brussels sprout's allies and friends.

A welcome departure from the usual oven-roasted sprouts, this salad is excellent tossed with the dressing 10 minutes before serving so that the raw sprouts have a chance to absorb some dressing and soften.

Serves 6–8

2 pounds brussels sprouts, ends trimmed and outer leaves removed
½ cup freshly grated Parmesan cheese, see instructions below
1 cup slivered or sliced almonds, toasted using Technique #1 (page 34)
Fresh Lemon Juice Dressing (page 33)
extra-virgin olive oil

Slice the brussels sprouts into thin circles or shave on a mandoline. Alternatively, if you have a food processor, you can fit it with the blade attachment and slice them that way. (This is the easiest way.) Set the sliced sprouts aside in a bowl.

Grate the Parmesan on the larger holes of a grater so that the pieces of cheese are similar in size to the shredded brussels sprouts.

Toss the toasted almonds and Parmesan with the sprouts. Add the dressing. Because the brussels sprouts are raw, it takes a decent amount of dressing to saturate the salad throughout so that it doesn't taste dry. Don't be shy; pour it on. Add more olive oil if you need to mellow out the tangy dressing.

Variations:

Use thinly shredded kale in addition to, or instead of, the brussels sprouts.

Use green or red cabbage instead of the brussels sprouts.

Use toasted pecans or pistachios instead of the almonds.

SHAVED CAULIFLOWER WITH PINE NUTS, CURRANTS, AND PARSLEY

Snow-white and flecked with dark currants and bright green parsley, this simple and festive winter salad is crunchy, sweet, sour, and salty—essentially all things I like. It is best to make the salad right before serving so that it is fresh and all the ingredients stand out, and to slice the cauliflower as thinly as possible. Always save a little parsley to sprinkle on at the end after you have finished tossing the salad.

Serves 6–8

1 small to medium head of cauliflower
½ cup raw pine nuts,
toasted using Technique #2 (page 34)
¼ cup black currants
1 handful of flat-leaf parsley leaves, coarsely chopped
Fresh Lemon Juice Dressing (page 33)
salt and freshly ground black pepper

Shave the cauliflower as thinly as possible, either on a mandoline (preferable) or carefully by hand. Toss with the toasted pine nuts, currants, and most of the parsley. Prepare the dressing and toss. Finish with a sprinkle of the remaining parsley and a few generous grindings of black pepper.

Variations:
Add another thinly sliced white vegetable, such as fennel, daikon radish, or turnips to the salad.

RED CABBAGE, PISTACHIO, AND MINT

This is one of those salads that has very few ingredients but really stands up to the heat. The cabbage serves as a fresh and crunchy platform for the herbs and nuts. This salad pairs well with just about anything, but I especially like it with spicy stews such as the Persian Chicken Stew (page 166) or the Braised Spiced Lamb with Yogurt and Walnuts (page 170).

Serves 8

1 medium head of red cabbage, outer leaves removed
1 cup raw pistachios, toasted using Technique #2 (page 34) and finely chopped
1 large handful of fresh mint leaves, finely chopped
extra-virgin olive oil
juice of 2 lemons
salt and freshly ground black pepper

Cut the cabbage into quarters. Laying each quarter flat side down, slice it as thinly as possible down to the core and discard the core. Place the sliced cabbage in a large bowl and dress it with just a little bit of olive oil and salt to taste. I find cabbage needs very little oil. Then dress with lots of lemon juice.

Gently toss the cabbage with the toasted pistachios and mint and season to taste with pepper. Serve immediately.

Variation:
This is Rosy Brown's favorite salad—try her variation with crumbled feta and currants soaked in lemon juice to make them nice and plump.

Aegina, Greece

GREEK FRIED EGGS

This is the only recipe for fried eggs that you will ever need. The trick is to spoon hot oil from the pan over the yolk until the top turns white. This makes for a perfectly cooked egg—the yellow is still runny, but the edges of the white are crispy and browned. Armed with this technique, you can channel your inner Greek mama, frying up eggs for a quick and easy dinner.

Per person:

2 eggs
extra-virgin olive oil
salt and freshly ground black pepper

Coat your frying pan (nonstick is best) with a good amount of olive oil—enough so that when you tilt your pan, you can easily dip your spoon to collect the oil. Heat the oil over medium-high heat for a minute and crack the eggs into the pan.

Allow the eggs to cook for a bit, until the whites are almost done and the edges are getting a little browned. Then tilt the pan and start spooning the hot oil over the yolks until they are just cooked on top. Sprinkle with salt and freshly ground black pepper and serve.

This page: Reggie, Mr. Keet, New York

Opposite page: Elizabeth Peyton and Matthew Barney, *The Hosts*, 2014

Soup from scratch is rarely something you make for just one person, so I tend to associate it with good company and family vibes. I like to serve soup as a main course, often building a menu around it, treating it like the star of the show. I'm sure this stems from how the Greeks serve soup. It is usually a main meal, the vegetarian soups served with some bread and cured fish, and the meat-based soups served with some bread and maybe a simple salad. Greek soups like *faki* and *revithia* are delicious and only need a few ingredients. Suddenly a lowly lentil or chickpea is transformed into a velvety, saucy soup that has you wondering if life is worth living past that moment. And then there are the thinner broth and vegetable soups I love just as much for their warming or cooling properties in their respective seasons. They are light, yet satisfying, and a perfect platform for bright colors and flavors.

SOUPS

KOTOSOUPA (GREEK CHICKEN SOUP WITH LEMON)

This is tangy, spicy, delicious chicken soup goodness. It is one of the most famous Greek recipes out there, and it tastes best when homemade. It will cure whatever illness or hangover you have, and if you have none, it will fend it off. Use a free-range chicken whenever possible.

Serves 6–8

Broth:
1 whole chicken (3–4 pounds) cut into 8 pieces
2 yellow onions, peeled and left whole
4 heads of garlic (leave the heads whole, or in pieces with the peel on, but cut off the root bottoms)
2 bay leaves
1 tablespoon whole black peppercorns
2 heaping teaspoons kosher salt

Soup:
1 of the cooked chicken breasts from the broth, shredded (or add more, if you'd like)
1 medium potato (any variety), peeled and diced
juice of 2 lemons
2 large eggs, beaten well
freshly ground black pepper
hot red pepper flakes
lemon wedges, for serving

To make the broth:

Rinse the chicken and take the skin off the thighs and one of the breasts. (I do this so that there isn't too much fat rendered out in the soup—you definitely want some though!)

Place the meat in a large, heavy-bottomed pot and fill with enough water to barely cover the chicken.

Add the whole onions, heads of garlic, bay leaves, peppercorns, and salt and bring to a boil.

Lower the heat to medium, cover the pot, and simmer for an hour.

Remove from the heat and pour the broth through a strainer set over a bowl. Remove the chicken and set it aside until it is cool enough to handle.

Clean and rinse out the pot you simmered the chicken and onions in and pour the broth back in. (I clean the pot so that any scum or dirt from the broth making disappears and the broth is nice and clear.)

Taste the broth for seasoning and add more salt if needed.

To make the soup:

Add the diced potato to the broth and simmer over medium heat for 5 or 6 minutes, until the potato is tender.

While the potato is simmering, shred one of the chicken breasts into small pieces. Reserve the rest of the chicken for chicken salad or something else. Add the shredded chicken to the soup and turn off the heat.

In a separate large bowl, whisk the lemon juice into the eggs. Now, you will temper the eggs so that they will not curdle in the broth.

Slowly whisk a ladleful of broth into the egg/lemon mixture. Repeat two more times and then slowly pour, while whisking, the egg/lemon mixture into the large pot of broth. Return the soup to medium-high heat and simmer once again, just for 30 or so seconds.

Sprinkle with hot red pepper flakes and freshly ground black pepper. Serve with extra lemon wedges on the side.

SPANISH-STYLE GAZPACHO

I learned this recipe in the kitchen of a Spanish family I lived with in Madrid for six weeks when I was fifteen years old. It is *the* summer soup, delicious and refreshing. The amount of vegetables does not need to be exact, but be sure to add enough olive oil so you have a nice creamy consistency. I would advise pouring the soup through a strainer after blending, as it makes for a much more velvety and refined gazpacho, but I often skip this step if I don't have the time. Both versions taste just as good.

Serves 4–6

8 ripe red tomatoes, beefsteak or heirloom variety
2 large seedless cucumbers, peeled
1 red or green bell pepper
¼ small red onion
1 garlic clove
2 slices of stale rustic bread, soaked in water for a minute (optional)
½ cup extra-virgin olive oil, plus more for serving
3 tablespoons balsamic vinegar
¼ cup water
salt and freshly ground black pepper
ice cubes, for serving

If you plan on straining your soup, set up a large mesh strainer over a large bowl.

Cut the tomatoes, cucumbers, pepper, and onion into large cubes and place in a bowl with the garlic and the soaked bread (if using). You will puree all the ingredients in a few batches in your blender using a small amount of the olive oil, vinegar, salt, and pepper each time.

Place the first batch of vegetables in the blender, add a third of the olive oil and balsamic vinegar, salt, pepper, and the entire ¼ cup of water to get the blender going. Blend until smooth.

Pour half of the first batch of blended soup into the bowl or strainer; you'll use the remaining half to get the second batch of vegetables going in the blender. Continue to blend in batches.

If you are straining the soup, use a spatula to move it around and push it through the strainer.

Taste for seasoning and add more salt or balsamic vinegar as needed.

Chill the soup in the fridge for at least an hour and then serve it in bowls with 1 or 2 ice cubes. Top the gazpacho with a splash of olive oil.

Make ahead: This soup is good for a couple of days in the refrigerator.

Variations:

Orange Gazpacho: *Follow the above ingredients and instructions but substitute yellow tomatoes for the red ones, an orange pepper for the green or red one, and boiled carrots for the cucumbers. (To prepare the carrots: Peel 4 large carrots and cut them into 1-inch-thick circles. Bring a small pot of salted water to a boil, add the carrots, simmering them in salted water until they are very soft; then drain and cool before blending.)*

Green Gazpacho: *Follow the above ingredients and instructions but substitute green heirloom tomatoes for the red ones, and a green bell pepper for the red pepper.*

ROOT VEGETABLE SOUP WITH PISTACHIO PARSLEY PESTO

This soup is a beauty. Depending on how you make it, the outcome is a striking galaxy of swirling red, green, and orange colors. Very simple, it makes the most out of the Northeast winter season, and is a nice, light alternative to the usual heavy meals we eat during this time. You can also use more of any one vegetable and make it a carrot soup, butternut squash soup, or sweet potato soup. The beets are optional, but I recommend making the effort if you're up for it because the visual outcome is so worth it!

Serves 6–8

Root Vegetable Soup:
2 yellow onions, diced
4 garlic cloves, coarsely chopped
1 small butternut squash, peeled, seeded, and diced
1 sweet potato, peeled and diced
1 potato, peeled and diced
2 carrots, diced
4 whole sprigs of fresh thyme
2 bay leaves
2 strips of orange peel
extra-virgin olive oil
2 red beets, peeled and diced (optional)
salt and freshly ground black pepper

Pistachio Parsley Pesto:
1 cup fresh flat-leaf parsley leaves
⅓ cup raw pistachios, shelled
zest of 1 lemon
1 garlic clove (optional)
¼ cup fresh lemon juice
⅓ cup extra-virgin olive oil
salt and freshly ground black pepper

To make the soup:
In a large pot over medium-low heat, sweat the onions and garlic in a generous coating of olive oil for about 5 minutes. Season with 2 generous pinches of salt and a grinding of black pepper.

Add the butternut squash, sweet potato, potato, and carrots to the pot along with the thyme sprigs and bay leaves. Add just enough cold water to barely cover the vegetables. (The trick here is not to use too much water—remember you can always add more later.)
Add the orange peel, raise the heat to high, and bring to a boil momentarily. Reduce the heat to medium-low and simmer uncovered for about 35 to 40 minutes until all the vegetables are nice and soft, stirring occasionally.
Remove the bay leaves, orange peel, and woody stems of the thyme and puree the soup in a blender or using an immersion blender. Add about ⅓ cup olive oil as you blend, to give the soup a lovely flavor and creamy consistency.
Before serving, top each bowl with a spoonful of the pesto.

To make the optional beet soup:
In a separate small pot, simmer two peeled and diced beets with barely enough water to cover them until they are soft and cooked through. Add a ladleful of soup from the other pot and puree the mixture in a food processor to make a second, bright red soup. Season with salt, black pepper, and olive oil. To serve, swirl a spoonful of the beet soup into the root vegetable soup for a colorful effect.

To make the pesto:
In a food processor, pulse the parsley, pistachios, lemon zest, garlic (if using), and lemon juice until just smooth. Pulse again, drizzling olive oil through the feed tube until the pesto is very smooth and bright green. Add a generous pinch of salt and freshly ground black pepper to taste.

RED LENTIL SOUP WITH CUMIN AND LIME

Is it wrong to have a deep-seated appreciation for health food? It's a secret I keep carefully tucked into my back pocket, but it informs almost everything I make . . . and even though I skip the tofu, tempeh, and seitan vibes of this world, I do appreciate a rich lentil soup as a base for fragrant spices and tangy lime.

Serves 6–8

1 16-ounce bag of red lentils
1 tablespoon unsalted butter
1 yellow onion, coarsely chopped
2 garlic cloves, coarsely chopped
1 bay leaf
2 teaspoons cumin seeds
1 teaspoon ground turmeric
1 jalapeño, coarsely chopped (optional)
extra-virgin olive oil
2 handfuls of fresh cilantro, finely chopped
salt and freshly ground black pepper
lime wedges, for serving

In a strainer, wash the lentils well and set aside.

In a large pot over medium heat, melt the butter and add the onion, garlic, bay leaf, cumin seeds, turmeric, and jalapeño (if using). Add a generous drizzle of olive oil and a generous pinch of salt.

Sauté until the onions are translucent and soft, 5 to 6 minutes, then add the washed lentils. Add enough water to the pot to cover the lentils by about 3 inches. Raise the heat and bring the soup to a boil momentarily. Reduce the heat to low and simmer, partially covered, until the lentils are very soft and breaking down on their own, about 30 to 40 minutes. If the soup is getting too thick, add more water, half a cup at a time.

Remove from heat and let the soup cool for about 15 minutes. Puree the soup using an immersion blender or a regular blender. Add another drizzle of olive oil and the chopped cilantro and briefly blend again.

Serve the soup warm with a drizzle of olive oil, a sprinkle of fresh pepper, and a lime wedge to squeeze on top.

Make ahead: This soup keeps great for a couple of days in the fridge.

Variation:

If you want the soup to be very spicy, add another chopped jalapeño or serrano pepper.

FAKI (GREEK LENTIL SOUP WITH CINNAMON AND CLOVES)

My yiayia, and most Greeks, traditionally make *faki* with lentils, onions, bay leaves, tomato puree, and water. I like to include cinnamon and cloves as well, to add depth and warmth. This soup is usually served with olives, smoked fish, and a hunk of feta. I also like to add an easy salad and some homemade hot sauce (page 154). Whatever you serve it with, the idea is to keep it simple.

Serves 6–8

1 large yellow onion, finely chopped
3 garlic cloves, finely chopped
1 pound green or black lentils, rinsed
2 whole bay leaves
1 cinnamon stick
2 whole cloves
1 teaspoon hot red pepper flakes
⅓ cup extra-virgin olive oil
1 14.5-ounce can of diced or pureed tomatoes
salt and freshly ground black pepper
2–3 tablespoons red wine vinegar (optional)

In a large pot over medium heat, sauté the onions and garlic with a generous drizzle of olive oil and a pinch of salt. Stir occasionally and sauté until the onions start to soften and become translucent, about 6 minutes.

Add the bay leaves, cinnamon stick, cloves, and pepper flakes to the onion and garlic. Sauté a minute longer until the spices become fragrant.

Add the lentils, tomatoes, and enough water so that the ingredients are covered by 3 inches of liquid in the pot. Turn the heat up to high and bring to a boil, then simmer the soup half-covered with a lid for about 40 minutes until the lentils are tender and the soup is thick. If you feel that the soup is too thick, add more water, a cup at a time.

When the soup has finished cooking, add another generous drizzle of olive oil at the end and stir to incorporate. (This is my grandma's trick—she likes the olive oil to be uncooked whenever possible.) Fish out the two bay leaves and discard.

Let the soup sit for 30 minutes and then taste it for seasoning.

I like *faki* plain, but others prefer it with vinegar or hot sauce. If you like, before serving you can add a couple of tablespoons of red wine vinegar or a dash of hot sauce.

Variations:

Leave out the cinnamon entirely and add a handful of chopped fresh flat-leaf parsley while you are sautéing the onions and garlic.

When tomatoes are in season, it is nice to use 4 large fresh ones, grated, instead of the canned tomatoes. To grate a tomato, hold it by the stem end and rub it against the coarse side of a grater set over a bowl. The skin will split open and you can grate the fleshy interior into pulp, leaving behind the tomato skin and stem, which you discard.

REVITHIA (CHICKPEA STEW WITH ROSEMARY, LEMON, AND OLIVE OIL)

This is my favorite stew, recipe courtesy of my yiayia. The day she told me she thought my chickpea stew was *nostimo* (tasty), I felt I had really accomplished something in life. The chickpeas cook until they are meltingly soft, and then they are drowned in olive oil and lots of lemon juice. After you have had this you don't ever want to eat anything else. It is a perfect example of Greek food at its best, transforming only a few ingredients into a luxurious meal.

Serves 6

1 16-ounce bag of dried (not canned) chickpeas
1 tablespoon baking soda
2 yellow onions, peeled and left whole
2 bay leaves
2 sprigs of fresh rosemary
4 tablespoons all-purpose flour
⅓ cup extra-virgin olive oil
juice of 1–2 lemons
salt and freshly ground black pepper

Soak the dried chickpeas in plenty of water overnight, or at least 6 hours.

When you are ready to make the stew, drain the chickpeas in a colander and rinse them well. Leaving them in the colander, dust the chickpeas with the baking soda (which serves as a tenderizer) and then toss to incorporate, using your hands.

Let the chickpeas sit for 30 minutes and then rinse very well, 3 or 4 times, in order to remove all the baking soda.

Place the chickpeas in large, heavy pot filled with enough water to cover them by two inches. Add the whole onions, the bay leaves, and a generous pinch of salt. Bring the stew to a boil, and then reduce the heat to low and cover.

After about 20 minutes, the chickpeas will start to give off a white froth. Skim this 2 or 3 times, and then don't worry about it.

After you've skimmed the stew a few times add 2 sprigs of fresh rosemary and simmer until the chickpeas are very tender, about another 40 minutes. Remove the onions and the rosemary sprigs.

To thicken the stew, place 4 tablespoons of flour in a mixing bowl and whisk it with ⅓ cup olive oil. Slowly drizzle in 2 cups of broth from the stew, whisking to remove any lumps.

Bring the stew to a low simmer. Add the flour mixture back to the pot, stirring well for about 3 minutes until the stew is thick and velvety.

Taste for seasoning and add more salt (you will most likely need to add another generous pinch or two) and freshly ground black pepper.

To serve, ladle into bowls and drizzle with olive oil and fresh lemon juice. This dish is best served on the day you make it.

Variation:

In the last 10 minutes of cooking, add 2 cups of cleaned and coarsely chopped chard or kale.

For a flourless version, omit the 4 tablespoons of flour and in a separate bowl combine 1 cup of the cooked chickpeas with 1 cup of broth. Using an immersion blender, puree to a smooth consistency and add back into the soup. Simmer the soup until it thickens a bit, about 10 to 15 minutes more. Puree another cup of chickpeas and broth if you like an even thicker consistency.

This page: Studio lunch, Mr. Keet, New York

Opposite page: Lunch with Yiayia, Piraeus, Greece

ivi
Loutraki

SPICY CHICKPEA STEW

I tried to make a tomato-based version of the lemony chickpea stew and I ended up with this. I like to pretend I invented it. Warming, spicy, and full of flavor, it's delicious with a spoonful of plain yogurt. You can adjust the heat to your taste, either using less or more of the jalapeño or serrano peppers.

Serves 8–10

1 16-ounce bag of dried chickpeas
1 tablespoon baking soda
1 large yellow onion, finely chopped
2 garlic cloves, finely chopped
1 jalapeño or serrano pepper, finely chopped
2 bay leaves
2 tablespoons cumin seeds
1 tablespoon ground coriander
2 teaspoons hot red pepper flakes
2 handfuls of fresh flat-leaf parsley, chopped, plus more for serving
1 28-ounce can of diced tomatoes
extra-virgin olive oil
salt and freshly ground black pepper
Greek yogurt, for serving

Soak the chickpeas in plenty of water overnight, or for least 6 hours. When you are ready to make the stew, drain the chickpeas in a colander and rinse them well. Leaving them in the colander, dust the chickpeas with the baking soda (which serves as a tenderizer) and then toss them to incorporate the baking soda, using your hands. Let the chickpeas sit for 30 minutes and then rinse them very well, 3 or 4 times, in order to remove all the baking soda.

Place the chickpeas in large, heavy pot filled with enough water to barely cover them. Bring the chickpeas to a boil and then reduce the heat to medium and simmer for about 20 minutes. The chickpeas will start to give off a white froth. Skim this 2 or 3 times, and then don't worry about it.

Cover and simmer until the chickpeas are very tender but not falling apart, about 30 to 40 more minutes.

Meanwhile, generously drizzle some olive oil into a medium sauté pan. Add the onions, garlic, and jalapeño or serrano pepper to the pan. Sauté over medium-high heat until everything is just starting to soften, about a minute or two. Add a generous pinch of salt and then add the bay leaves, cumin seeds, coriander, hot red pepper flakes, and chopped parsley.

Sauté the onion mixture until it is soft and aromatic, about 5 minutes. Add the diced tomatoes and stir, cooking sauce for another 5 minutes.

When the chickpeas are done, remove enough of the cooking water so that the top layer of chickpeas is dry (think 2 inches of water below the chickpeas). Add the onion/tomato mixture to the chickpeas and give a good stir. There should be just enough liquid to barely cover the top of the chickpeas; add more water if necessary.

Simmer for about 30 minutes so that all the ingredients meld together. Let the stew cool for a few minutes and then add ⅓ cup olive oil, stirring to combine. Taste for seasoning, adding more salt and freshly ground black pepper as needed.

Serve with a spoonful of Greek yogurt and a sprinkle of parsley in every bowl.

Makeshift sink, Amagansett, New York

This page: Yiayia's garden, Aegina, Greece

Opposite page: Rob Pruitt, *Studio Stew*, 2014

In the United States, people tend to think of vegetables as a side, but I grew up eating vegetables as main dishes, cooked the Greek way—braised long and slow, in tomato sauce or lemon juice with oh-so-very-much olive oil. I treat vegetables with the same, if not more, reverence that I do meat. With their variety of colors, textures, and shapes, I find them endlessly inspiring, and, hey, they make you feel good to boot. As I've mentioned before, I firmly believe that the olive oil is as important as the dish's main ingredient; they sit side by side, creating perfect harmony and flavor.

In addition to braising, I also like to prepare vegetables by roasting them with lots of olive oil and salt in a hot oven until they are all caramelized and sweet. This technique is very easy—all it takes is patience.

VEGETABLES

AGINARES ME ARAKA (BRAISED ARTICHOKES, PEAS, AND POTATOES IN LEMON AND OLIVE OIL)

This is one of my favorite springtime dishes, although I have to admit that I've been known to make it in the dead of winter, using frozen artichokes and peas. *Aginares me Araka* is heaven in a pot: the vegetables are cooked with scallions, dill, and just a bit of olive oil until very soft, and then, at the very end, are drowned in lemon juice and lots more olive oil. It's best to add the majority of the olive oil just before serving, so you can taste its full flavor. I can't stress how important it is to use a good-quality extra-virgin olive oil in this (and all your food). It makes a huge difference.

Serves 4–6

juice of 2 lemons (or more, to taste)
6 artichoke hearts, fresh or frozen
extra-virgin olive oil
1 bunch of scallions, chopped, white and light-green parts only
2 handfuls of fresh dill, chopped
2 medium waxy potatoes, each cut into 8 chunks
2 cups peas, fresh or frozen
2 teaspoons all-purpose flour
salt and freshly ground black pepper

Squeeze the juice of 1 lemon into a medium bowl of water. If using fresh artichokes, clean them by cutting off their bases removing the leaves, and cleaning out the fuzzy "choke" area with a spoon so that you are left with only the hearts. Slice them into quarters and toss them in the lemon water. If using frozen artichokes, you can skip this step.

Pour about 3 tablespoons of olive oil in a medium pot and add the scallions, one handful of the dill, and a generous pinch of salt and a grinding of black pepper. Sauté over medium-high heat until everything is just wilted, about 3 to 5 minutes.

Remove the artichokes from the lemon water and add them and the potatoes to the pot. Pour in just enough fresh water to barely cover the artichokes and potatoes. Go for less rather than more, because you can always add a bit more water if you find there isn't enough. If using frozen artichoke hearts, add them to the pot whole, as is.

Simmer over low heat with the lid on for 15 to 20 minutes, until the artichokes and potatoes are tender. If using frozen artichokes, remove them from the pot and cut them into quarters and place back in the pot.

Add the peas and the second handful of dill, covering the pot again and shaking it to distribute everything. (I add the dill in two batches because I think it is a nice combination to have some of the dill mellow and cooked, and then some fresh bright flavor from the newly added herb.)

Simmer for about 5 more minutes. Take the pot off the heat and douse with more olive oil. (Go for it, really.)

Squeeze the juice of the second lemon into a separate bowl (you can also add more lemon here if you like things very tangy), and add the 2 teaspoons of flour. Stir to combine so there are no lumps, adding a splash of liquid from the pot if needed to loosen up the mixture.

Add the lemon/flour mixture to the pot, and shake the pot again to distribute. Cook over low heat for just another minute. At this point you should have a creamy sauce that just covers all the vegetables. If it is too thick, add a bit more water.

Serve as a main course with good bread and olives.

FASOLAKIA (BRAISED GREEN BEANS IN TOMATO AND OLIVE OIL)

This is a healthy, cheap, and easy one-pot meal. Green beans are braised until very tender and then soaked in olive oil. They should be cooked until the contents of the pot change from bright red and green to more muted tones, and until the beans are on the verge of falling apart. This dish requires good bread, maybe some feta or yogurt, and some cured fish.

Serves 4–6

1 large yellow onion, chopped
extra-virgin olive oil
1 pound green beans, ends trimmed
1 bay leaf
1 14.5-ounce can of crushed tomatoes or 4 fresh tomatoes, grated
salt and freshly ground black pepper

In a large pot, sauté the onions over medium-low heat in enough olive oil to generously coat them and a generous pinch of salt. When the onions are soft and translucent, add the green beans, the bay leaf, the tomatoes, and just enough water to barely cover the beans.

Simmer for about an hour, stirring occasionally and adding just a bit of water if it seems like there isn't enough. The beans are done when they have no snap to them and are very soft and saucy. After you remove the pot from the heat, add another generous drizzle of olive oil and season with salt and pepper to taste.

Variations:

Around 20 minutes into the cooking, add a potato, peeled and cut into wedges. Keep in mind that potatoes take longer to cook in a tomato base. Make sure to try one and check for tenderness.

Around 30 minutes into the cooking, add some pieces of chicken. I like using skinless thighs or breasts. Simmer the green beans with the chicken for about 30 minutes, until the chicken is cooked through.

Experiment with adding different spices. When you are sautéing the onions, add a tablespoon of ground cumin, ground coriander, finely minced fresh ginger, or a combination of all three.

GRILLED RAMPS WITH CRUSHED HAZELNUTS AND LEMON

Ramps are the best of part of early spring, and make everyone crazy with excitement. I must admit, these wild leeks are pretty delicious. Since they are only in season for a short period of time, let them be the star. Grilled ramps are perfect alongside "Grilled" Whole Fish (page 141) or Seared Duck Breast (page 160).

Serves 4–6

1 pound ramps, ends cut off and washed well (they tend to be very dirty things)
extra-virgin olive oil
⅓ cup raw hazelnuts, toasted using Technique #1 (page 34) and finely chopped
juice of 1 lemon
salt and freshly ground black pepper

Drizzle the ramps with olive oil and grill over medium-hot coals until they are charred. Alternatively, you can sear the ramps in a frying pan over medium-high heat. If you have smaller ramps they will be perfectly cooked throughout. If you have bigger ramps, wrap the leaves in aluminum foil and grill the white part first, later unwrapping the leaves to grill them as well.

Place the grilled ramps on a platter and drizzle them with more olive oil and sprinkle with the chopped hazelnuts. Dress them with the lemon juice and season with salt and black pepper. Serve warm or at room temperature.

ROASTED ACORN SQUASH WITH THYME

The key to a perfectly roasted vegetable is knowing your oven and using enough olive oil. Every oven is a little different and burns a bit differently as well. You really can't go wrong with roasting at 400 °F, but if you feel that it's taking too long to get a golden color on your veggies, turn it up to 425 °F. Roasting vegetables shouldn't take longer than around 40 minutes.

The other trick to making a nice caramelized vegetable is using enough olive oil for the vegetables to soak up. I find that when people get confused about how to get their vegetables roasted and delicious, they have usually skimped on the olive oil. In this recipe there should be a thin layer all over the baking sheet for the squash to lie in. Keep cooking until you flip a piece of squash and see that the face-down side is turning golden brown—then, and only then, take them out of the oven.

Serves 6–8

3 acorn squashes, washed, halved and seeds scraped out
extra-virgin olive oil
4 or 5 sprigs of fresh thyme
salt and freshly ground black pepper

Preheat the oven to 400 °F.

Cut the ends off each squash half and then cut each half into 1-inch smiles. Toss the squash pieces with a generous amount of olive oil and place them on a baking sheet (lined with parchment paper, if you want to make clean-up easier). Drizzle a little more olive oil over the squash and then sprinkle with salt and pepper. Moisten the thyme sprigs with a bit of olive oil as well, and then drape them over the squash.

Roast for about 45 minutes, until the side facing down is golden brown and the squash is fork-tender. Remove the thyme sprigs, shaking them a bit to release the leaves onto the squash.

You can absolutely eat the skin.

Variations:

Try roasting romesco, broccoli, carrots, butternut squash, sweet potatoes, or fennel all in the same way. Eggplants, cut into half-inch medallions, are also very nice, but make sure to add even more olive oil, as eggplants are like sponges, and if you don't use enough oil they will come out dry.

Roast the vegetables with different spices such as hot red pepper flakes, fennel seeds, mustard seeds, or cumin seeds. Chopped fresh garlic and ginger are also delicious. For example, sweet potatoes are especially wonderful with ginger and/or sesame seeds and eggplant pairs well with garlic, hot red pepper flakes, and parsley.

After the vegetables are roasted, try sprinkling them with chopped fresh herbs such as flat-leaf parsley, mint, or cilantro.

Sprinkle the roasted vegetables with toasted sesame seeds. Toast the sesame seeds in a dry pan over low heat, stirring often until golden brown.

ROASTED CAULIFLOWER AND CAULIFLOWER LEAVES WITH SPICES

This is delicious served with Tahini Dressing (page 33). I like to spread a thick layer of tahini on the plate, top it with the roasted cauliflower, and finish with more tahini and a sprinkle of parsley. Plain, however, also can't be beat.

Serves 4

1 head of cauliflower
extra-virgin olive oil
a sprinkle of hot red pepper flakes
a sprinkle of fennel seeds
a generous sprinkle of cumin seeds
salt and freshly ground black pepper
1 handful of fresh flat-leaf parsley (optional)

Preheat the oven to 400 °F.

Wash and dry the cauliflower. Cut off about half an inch from the bottom, and remove and discard any wilting leaves. Peel off any crisp and fresh cauliflower leaves from the base and reserve.

Coarsely chop the cauliflower, trying to keep the integrity of the florets. Alternatively you could make cauliflower "steaks" by cutting the entire head into half-inch-thick slices.

Place the cauliflower on a baking sheet (lined with parchment paper, if you want to make clean-up easier). Drizzle with olive oil (use more than you think you'll need). Sprinkle on the spices, salt, and pepper. Toss the reserved leaves with olive oil and salt and place in a corner of the roasting pan as they will cook quicker.

Roast the cauliflower until golden brown, about 40 minutes. The leaves will be done after 30 minutes and should be deliciously crisp.

Sprinkle with fresh parsley leaves (if using) and serve.

ROASTED FETA, PEPPERS, AND TOMATOES

This is one of those dishes that is as good as the ingredients you put in it. Use good produce, good feta, and good olive oil. Cook it until you see the feta and the peppers starting to brown, and some delicious olive-oil-y juices gathering at the bottom of the pan.

Serves 4–6

6 Anaheim peppers
a hunk of French or Greek feta (about ¾ cup, crumbled)
2 ripe tomatoes, coarsely chopped
extra-virgin olive oil
a generous pinch of dried oregano
salt and freshly ground black pepper

Preheat the oven to 425 °F.

Slice the peppers down the middle lengthwise and remove the seeds. Place on a baking sheet or in a roasting pan, skin side down. Sprinkle the crumbled feta and tomatoes over the peppers.

Drizzle with lots of olive oil and sprinkle with a generous pinch of oregano and a pinch of salt and a grinding of black pepper.

Roast in the oven for 30 to 40 minutes, or until everything starts to brown.

This dish is best served right out of the oven with a drizzle of extra olive oil and fresh bread.

Variations:

Add sliced jalapeños, thinly sliced red onion and a handful of fresh flat-leaf parsley leaves before baking.

Include sliced potatoes along with the peppers, adding 3 tablespoons of water to the bottom of the pan before baking, which transforms this dish into a main course.

ROASTED CARROTS WITH AVOCADO, CILANTRO, AND LIME

This dish is always a favorite. The roasted carrots are soft, sweet, and caramelized, while the avocado makes it rich and satisfying.

Serves 4–6

8–10 large carrots, scrubbed well (peeled if very dirty) and sliced on the diagonal ½ inch thick
extra-virgin olive oil
a generous sprinkle of ground cumin (you want a light dusting on every carrot)
a generous sprinkle of fennel seeds
a sprinkle of hot red pepper flakes
1–2 ripe avocados, sliced
juice of 1 lime
1 handful of fresh cilantro leaves
salt and freshly ground black pepper
1 handful of arugula or other pretty greens (optional)

Preheat the oven to 400 °F.

Generously drizzle the carrots with olive oil and place them on a baking sheet. Dust the carrots with the cumin and fennel seeds, and sprinkle with the hot red pepper flakes, salt, and pepper.

Roast the carrots in the oven until they are crispy on the edges but soft in the middle, about 45 minutes.

When the carrots are done roasting, place them on a serving platter, and scatter the sliced avocado and cilantro leaves on top. Drizzle with olive oil, a sprinkle of salt, and the lime juice.

If using arugula or another green, arrange it on top of the carrots and avocado, and dress with another drizzle of olive oil and a sprinkle of salt and pepper.

Make ahead: You can roast the carrots ahead of time (they will be good for about an hour) and keep them covered in a warm oven until you're ready to serve.

SMASHED CRISPY POTATOES

These little potatoes are almost better than french fries. They are crispy, soft, salty, trustworthy, reliable, attractive, and everything you really want out of a spud.

Serves 4–6

2 pounds small "new" potatoes, red-skinned or yellow-skinned (think 3–4 potatoes per person)
extra-virgin olive oil
2 sprigs of fresh rosemary
a pinch of dried oregano
salt and freshly ground black pepper

Preheat the oven to the highest setting on your broiler, or 450 °F. Place the rack two levels away from the broiler. Line a baking sheet with aluminum foil and pour a generous drizzle of olive oil on top.

Bring a large pot of heavily salted water to a boil.

Drop the potatoes in the water, and boil them until just cooked through, about 20 minutes. Drain and let them cool. Place the potatoes one at a time on a cutting board, and crush them just a bit with the bottom of a glass or the flat side of a knife.

Transfer the potatoes to the baking sheet and don't worry if the potatoes fall apart—that just creates more surface area, which means more crispy goodness.

Drizzle the potatoes with more olive oil, and sprinkle them with oregano, salt and pepper.

Tuck the rosemary sprigs in between the potatoes, wherever they fit.

If you're using the broiler, place the potatoes in the oven and broil them until they are crispy, 5 to 7 minutes. Alternatively, roast the potatoes at 450 °F for 20 minutes.

BEET FRITTERS

Nothing seems to excite people more than a freshly fried fritter. Beet fritters bridge the worlds of "healthy vegetable" and "fried little delight." Their bright red color and sweet flavor reminds you they are made of beets, but their crunchy fried texture delivers all the pleasure of delicious shoestring potatoes.

Makes 18–20

1 pound red beets, scrubbed clean and coarsely grated (about 3–4 medium beets)
1 large russet potato, peeled and coarsely grated
1 large egg
4 tablespoons all-purpose flour
2 handfuls of fresh mint, chopped
salt and freshly ground black pepper
frying oil (safflower, canola, and vegetable oil all work well)

Place the grated beets in a colander and toss with a sprinkle of salt. Press down on the beets to drain excess liquid. Then, you can spread them out on paper towels and try to get them as dry as possible.

Place the grated potato in a bowl of cold water and let it soak while the beets are drying. This removes some of the starch from the potato and allows the fritter to get crispier during frying.

Scoop out the grated potato from the bowl with your hands. Blot the potatoes with paper towels to dry, and add to a clean bowl along with the beets.

Add the egg and beat to incorporate with the beet mixture. Add the flour, the chopped mint, a generous pinch of salt and a few generous grindings of black pepper. The mixture should just hold together when you pinch it with your fingers.

Heat about ¼ inch of oil in a large nonstick frying pan over medium-high heat. Make sure the oil is nice and hot, and then working in two batches, drop ¼ cup of the fritter mixture into the pan. Flatten very gently, if at all. When you see the edges are crispy, about 3 to 4 minutes, flip the fritters and fry on the other side. Remove the fritters and place on a paper towel lined plate. Season with another sprinkle of salt, and serve.

Variations:

Replace one of the beets with 2 grated carrots to make beet-and-carrot fritters.

Add 2 teaspoons of cumin seeds to the beet mixture before frying for a slightly different flavor.

This page: *Lotti's Garden*, Los Angeles, California

Opposite page: Cyril eating pasta, Los Angeles, California

Pasta, for me, is an intimate experience. I never cook it for a crowd, and I usually eat it with family. The best pasta I have ever had has always been in someone's home, and never the fancy stuff in a restaurant. All of my pasta recipes lend themselves to simple, cozy, and quick meals at home.

PASTA

MAKARONIA ME KIMA (CINNAMON AND CLOVE MEAT RAGU)

When my mother and I get together, this is what we eat. We both get just as excited about it, and make it for each other when one of us is coming to visit. *Parigoria* in Greek means "to console"—when things are less than perfect, the consolation, or *parigoria,* is this dinner. It is a special meat sauce; aromatic with cinnamon and cloves, it fills your kitchen with the most wonderful smell.

Serves 4

1 medium yellow onion, finely chopped
extra-virgin olive oil
1 cinnamon stick
3 whole cloves
1 bay leaf
a pinch of hot red pepper flakes
1 pound ground beef
1 14.5-ounce can of pureed tomatoes
1 pound pasta of your choice
salt and freshly ground black pepper
Parmesan cheese, for serving

In a medium pot, sauté the onion with a generous drizzle of olive oil, a generous pinch of salt, and a grinding of black pepper over medium-low heat just for a minute before adding the cinnamon stick, cloves, bay leaf, and hot pepper flakes. Continue to sauté until the onions are translucent and soft, about 5 to 6 minutes.

Raise the heat to medium-high and add the ground beef, breaking it into small chunks with a wooden spoon and sautéing for about 5 minutes.

Add the tomatoes and simmer for about 40 minutes on low heat. When it has cooled down, taste and adjust the seasoning as needed.

Cook the pasta in plenty of salted boiling water until al dente, and drain. Drizzle with olive oil and a pinch of salt, tossing the pasta to distribute. Serve the ragù over the pasta with freshly grated Parmesan on the side.

EGG NOODLES WITH GARLIC, CHILI, LEMON ZEST, AND PARSLEY

Greek egg noodles, known as *hilopites*, come in many different shapes and sizes. I prefer the long, noodle-shaped *hilopites*. They are delicious, and have a different bite and flavor than regular egg noodles because they are made with milk, rather than water.
You should be able to find *hilopites* at any Greek or Armenian grocery store, or you can use regular egg noodles instead. I like this dish without any cheese, but if you want to make it richer, Parmesan or *Kefalograviera* (a Greek hard cheese often served with pasta) would be a tasty addition.

Serves 4–6

3 or 4 garlic cloves, finely chopped
extra-virgin olive oil
1–2 teaspoons hot red pepper flakes, depending on how spicy you like it
zest of 1 lemon
1 pound Greek egg noodles
1 bunch of fresh flat-leaf parsley, finely chopped
salt and freshly ground black pepper
***Kefalograviera* or Parmesan cheese, grated (optional)**

In a large pan, add the garlic and the olive oil (3 tablespoons should be enough to generously coat the bottom of the pan). Cook the garlic over a low flame for about 2 minutes. It shouldn't color at all, but rather soften and infuse the olive oil with flavor. Add the hot pepper flakes and lemon zest with a generous pinch of salt.

In a pot of salted water, boil the noodles until al dente. Drain, and place them in the pan with the garlic, pepper flakes, and lemon zest. Toss to incorporate and add the chopped parsley. Taste for seasoning and add more salt, hot pepper flakes, and black pepper as needed. Serve as is or with freshly grated *Kefalograviera* or Parmesan cheese.

ORZO WITH BLACK PEPPER, PINE NUTS, AND BUTTER

Orzo is delicious, but requires a little attention to cook it properly. You can make it exactly like pasta, bringing a pot of salted water to a rolling boil, cooking the orzo to al dente, and draining it. Or, you can cook it like rice, adding just enough liquid so the orzo absorbs it all.

This is lovely with a braised meat like *Kokkinisto* (page 164). You can serve the saucy meat right on top of the orzo, sprinkling it with extra Parmesan to serve.

Serves 4–6

1 pound orzo
3 tablespoons unsalted butter
extra-virgin olive oil
1 tablespoon freshly ground black pepper
1 cup Parmesan cheese, freshly grated (or more, to taste)
½ cup raw pine nuts, toasted using Technique #2 (page 34)
salt

Cook the orzo in plenty of salted boiling water until al dente. Stir it often so it doesn't stick. Drain the orzo and return it to the pot.

Add the butter and a sprinkle of salt (about a teaspoon) to the pot and gently toss until the butter melts.

Let the orzo cool just a bit and then you can gauge how much olive oil to add. If it is still very sticky, add a generous drizzle; if it is not that sticky, you can add a bit less.

Toss the orzo with the black pepper, Parmesan, and toasted pine nuts. Serve warm.

Top: Yiayia's kitchen, Aegina, Greece. Bottom: Orange trees, Piraeus, Greece

Piraeus, Greece

This page: Lunch at The Geffen Contemporary at MOCA, Los Angeles, California

Opposite page: Alex Eagleton, *Sometimes Always*, 2014

Before I started cooking full-time, I had a clothing line that occupied most of my time. My interest in Persian food was sparked after many years of working with an Iranian patternmaker named Houshang Mohseni, who would occasionally take me out to lunch at the Persian restaurants in Midtown. I would then bring him Greek desserts like baklava and we would chat about how much our cultures have in common.

I find that what Persians do with rice is something akin to perfection, combining textures, colors, and aromatics in ways I never thought possible. Much of my inspiration comes from Iran when dealing with rice. Although I can't definitively say that any of these rice dishes are traditionally Persian in any way, the spirit is there.

GRAINS AND PULSES

SAFFRON RICE

Saffron is a luxurious addition to rice, infusing it with fragrance and color. I like to place the saffron threads in the pot along with the rice, lots of butter, and bay leaves. Doing it this way creates speckled shades of deep yellows and orange colors and makes the dish really stand out on your table. Saffron rice pairs perfectly with stews and braised meats.

Serves 6

2 cups basmati rice, rinsed in cold water at least 5 times, until the water starts to run clear
3 tablespoons unsalted butter
1 teaspoon salt
2 bay leaves
2 pinches of saffron threads

Place the rinsed rice in a pot with 3½ cups of cold water and add the remaining ingredients on top. Bring the water to a boil.

Reduce the heat to a simmer and cover with a lid that has been wrapped in a kitchen towel so that the towel is inside your pot on the bottom of the lid. (This will absorb the steam and make the rice fluffier.) Cook over low heat for about 20 minutes or until all the water is absorbed. Fluff with a fork and serve.

TAH-DIG WITH PISTACHIOS, APRICOTS, AND CARAMELIZED ONIONS

Tah-dig, meaning "bottom of the pot" in Farsi, refers to the crispy golden crust of rice found at the bottom of the pot after cooking. This is my own interpretation of a dressed up *tah-dig.* What's more Persian (and Greek, for that matter) than pistachios and apricots? This dish is a beauty, not to mention a savory and sweet combination to die for.

Serves 4–6

4 tablespoons unsalted butter, plus more as necessary
1 small yellow onion, chopped
½ cup dried apricots, cut into slivers
¾ cup raw pistachios, shelled, toasted using Technique #2 (page 34), and chopped
2 cups long-grain rice (such as basmati or jasmine)
1–2 tablespoons extra-virgin olive oil
¾ cup hot water
salt

In a skillet, melt 2 tablespoons of the butter and add the onion along with a generous pinch of salt. Sauté over medium heat until the onion is soft and lightly browned. Add the apricots and sauté a bit longer just until they deepen in color. Remove from heat to a plate and cool. Add chopped pistachios to the apricot/onion mixture and set aside.

In a large saucepan, bring 8 cups of water and 1 tablespoon of salt to a boil. You are going to parboil the rice as if it were pasta. When the water comes to a boil, add the rice and stir so it doesn't stick together. Parboil the rice for 6 minutes—no more, no less—and then drain the rice in a mesh colander and rinse it immediately with lots of cold water.

In a large nonstick skillet with a lid (I use a heavy plate as a lid), melt the remaining 2 tablespoons of the butter and 1 tablespoon of olive oil over medium-high heat. Carefully spoon the parboiled rinsed rice into the middle of the pan, and then gently spread it out to the sides. Poke holes in the rice with the handle of your spoon and sprinkle it with a pinch of salt. Add ½ cup water and reduce the heat to low.

Wrap a clean, dry kitchen towel around the bottom of the lid, tucking it in at the handle. (The towel should cover the lid on the inside of the pan and will absorb the steam so it does not drip down into the rice.)

Secure the lid as tightly as you can on the skillet. Cook over low heat for about 10 minutes, and then check the rice by tasting a few grains to see if they are done. If they are, remove the lid. If not, add a bit more water, 2 tablespoons at a time, and cover the skillet again.

When the rice is done, scatter half of the pistachio/apricot/onion mixture over the skillet, gently pushing it into the holes you made in the rice. Turn the heat to medium-high until you see the edges of the rice are turning golden brown. I like to drizzle a bit more melted butter or olive oil around the edge of the pan to help move things along.

Remove the skillet from the heat and let it cool. (You can also fill your sink with an inch of cold water and place the bottom of the pan in the sink. This helps the *tah-dig* to unstick, although if you have a good nonstick pan this shouldn't be a problem.)

When you are ready to serve, flip the *tah-dig* by holding a serving plate face-down against the skillet and turning the skillet upside down on the plate. Don't worry if the crust falls apart; it will still taste good. Sprinkle the remaining pistachio/apricot/onion mixture on top and serve.

TAH-DIG WITH POTATO CRUST

Tah-dig with potato crust is one of my favorites. You will be so proud of yourself when you accomplish flipping the finished dish potato-side up that you might never need to do anything else in your life. If you don't succeed and it falls apart, don't despair—just layer the pieces of crispy potato over the rice and keep pursuing your dreams!

Serves 6

2 cups long-grain rice (such as basmati or jasmine)
2 Yukon Gold potatoes, peeled
4 tablespoons unsalted butter
2 tablespoons extra-virgin olive oil
¾ cup hot water
salt

In a large saucepan, bring 6 cups of water and 1 tablespoon of salt to a boil. When the water comes to a boil, add the rice and stir so that it doesn't stick together. Parboil the rice for 6 minutes—no more, no less—and then drain the rice in a mesh colander and rinse it immediately with lots of cold water.

Slice the potatoes very thinly on a mandoline or as thin as you can get them by hand.

In a large lidded nonstick pan over medium heat, melt 2 tablespoons of the butter and 1 tablespoon of the olive oil. Add the potato slices and spread them out in a single layer, pushing them up along the sides of the pan slightly. Season with a sprinkle of salt.

Carefully spoon the parboiled rice into the middle of the pan, and then gently spread it out to the sides. Poke holes in the rice with the handle of your spoon. Pour ¾ cup hot water over the rice and reduce the heat to low.

Wrap a clean, dry kitchen towel around the bottom of the lid, tucking it in at the handle. (The towel should cover the lid on the inside of the pan and will absorb the steam so it does not drip down into the rice.) Secure the lid as tightly as you can on the skillet. Cook for 10 minutes.

Lift the lid and taste a bit of rice from the center of the pan. If it is not fully cooked, add just a bit more water, 2 tablespoons at a time. You want to create more steam rather than end up with extra water.

In another pan, melt the remaining 2 tablespoons of butter, add to the rice along with a pinch of salt and replace the lid. Check every 5 minutes until the rice is cooked and you see the edges of the potatoes getting crispy. If the rice is cooked but you see the potatoes are still white, remove the lid and turn the heat up to medium-high in order to crisp it up.

Drizzle the remaining tablespoon of olive oil around the edge of the *tah-dig* while it is still in the pan.

Remove from the heat and wait for it to cool down a bit. This will also help the crust to unstick from the bottom of the pan.

Now, the tricky part: place a serving plate face-down on the skillet and flip them both in one strong motion so the *tah-dig* is on a plate with the potato crust side up. If the crust separates from the rice, or breaks apart, do not fret; just drape it over the top of rice. It will taste just as good.

MUJADDARA (RICE AND LENTILS WITH FRIED ONIONS)

This is my take on a dish that is popular throughout the Arab world. What makes it extraordinarily tasty is the fried onions. Comforting and hearty, it is lovely served as a vegetarian main with a simple salad and Tahini Dressing (page 33). I also like to add sliced avocado on top when serving.

Serves 6–8

1 cup French lentils (you can also use brown lentils)
1 cup basmati rice, rinsed in cold water at least 5 times, until the water starts to run clear
2 tablespoons unsalted butter, divided
3 tablespoons extra-virgin olive oil
1 bay leaf
2 large yellow onions, sliced into ¼-inch half-moons
salt and freshly ground black pepper
2 sliced avocados, for serving
Tahini Dressing (page 33)

Bring a pot of salted water to a boil, add the lentils, and turn the heat to medium-low, simmering until tender, about 20 to 25 minutes. Drain the lentils and toss them with a generous drizzle of olive oil.

While the lentils are cooking, place another medium pot over high heat and pour in 2 cups of cold water, a tablespoon of butter, and a pinch of salt and add the rice. Bring to a boil, and then cover, reducing the heat to low. Simmer until all of the water is absorbed, about 10 to 12 minutes. Fluff the rice with a fork, and set aside.

In a skillet, heat a generous drizzle of olive oil (about 3 tablespoons), 1 tablespoon of butter, and the bay leaf over medium-high heat. Add the onions to the skillet with a generous pinch of salt and a grinding of black pepper. Cook the onions until they soften, about 5 to 6 minutes. Reduce the heat to medium-low and continue to cook, stirring occasionally, until the onions are very soft and have a golden caramel color with dark, crispy parts, about 15 to 20 minutes, adjusting the heat as necessary to achieve this.

Turn off the heat, and add the lentils and the rice to the fried onions. The moisture from the rice and lentils will deglaze the pan of all the lovely toasty bits. Taste for seasoning, adding more salt and pepper as needed. Serve with sliced avocado on top and Tahini Dressing on the side.

GREEK *FAVA* (YELLOW LENTILS WITH LEMON AND OLIVE OIL)

In Greece, this smooth and creamy side dish of yellow lentils is usually served with fish or as a mezze with ouzo. It is topped with lots of olive oil, lemon juice, and chopped red onion or capers. It is always a crowd-pleaser, and is very simple to make once you get the consistency down.

Serves 6–8

1 pound yellow lentils, rinsed very well (you can also use yellow split peas)
1 yellow onion, peeled and left whole
2 bay leaves
extra-virgin olive oil
fresh lemon juice
salt and freshly ground black pepper
½ red onion, thinly sliced or finely chopped (optional)
salt-packed capers (optional)

Place the lentils, onion, and bay leaves in a pot and add water to cover the lentils by an inch. (It's okay if the onion is skimming the surface.) Bring to a boil, and then reduce to a simmer. You will need to stand by the pot and skim off any froth that rises to the surface. Add 2 teaspoons of salt, and simmer the lentils for about 35 to 45 minutes until the mixture starts to thicken. What you are trying to do is simmer them until they soften and resemble a thick soup. You might need to add a bit more water during the cooking process to keep it somewhat loose. One thing to keep in mind is that *fava* continues to thicken considerably after it has cooled down.

When the lentils have finished cooking, remove the onion and bay leaves and add ¼ cup of extra-virgin olive oil. Use an immersion blender or a food processor to puree the mixture. I do not like a completely smooth *fava*, and if you process it too much, it will become gummy, so go easy. You are looking for a smooth puree (think the consistency of hummus) but if it's a little chunky, that's okay too.

Spread the *fava* on a platter, drizzle with lots of olive oil and fresh lemon juice, and scatter a few slices of red onion and the capers (if using) on top. Serve the *fava* warm, or at room temperature.

FALAFEL PARTY

Falafel is homemade fast food that makes the ultimate sandwich. I like to make falafel heavy on the herbs so it is vibrantly green after frying. The falafel comes out crispy on the outside, soft and infused with cilantro, mint, and parsley on the inside. Another great part about a falafel-fest is that the fixings are almost as fun as the falafel themselves—tahini sauce, labne (a rich and thick Middle-Eastern yogurt), your favorite hummus recipe, sliced pickles, and red cabbage. It's a completely balanced meal, all stuffed in pita bread. As my dad likes to say, "It's falafenomenal."

Serves 6–8
makes about 16 balls

Falafel:
1 pound dried chickpeas, soaked overnight in plenty of water
1 small yellow onion, roughly chopped
2 garlic cloves
1 large handful of fresh flat-leaf parsley, roughly chopped (stems included)
1 large handful of fresh cilantro, roughly chopped (stems included)
1 handful of fresh mint, leaves only
2 teaspoons ground cumin
2 teaspoons ground coriander
¼ teaspoon cayenne pepper
2 tablespoons all-purpose flour
salt and freshly ground black pepper
frying oil (safflower, canola, and vegetable oil all work well)

To serve:
Pita bread
Tahini Dressing (page 33)
Greek yogurt or Labne
Hummus
Pickles
Shredded cabbage

Drain the chickpeas and pulse them in a food processor with the onion, garlic, parsley, cilantro, mint, cumin, coriander, and cayenne pepper to form a coarse meal. Transfer to a bowl and sprinkle the flour over the mixture. Stir to just incorporate and then generously season with salt and pepper.

Refrigerate the mixture for 1 to 2 hours.

Make a "test ball" out of the falafel mixture—I like to make them about the size of a slightly flattened golf ball, but you can make them more round or more flat if you'd like.

The falafel mixture should come together easily when you try to form a ball, and stay together during frying. Use a gentle hand when forming your balls and don't overwork the mixture, as this will lead to a heavy falafel.

In a frying pan over medium-high heat, pour about an inch of oil and fry your "test ball." If it falls apart, add more flour to the falafel mixture, about a tablespoon.

Fry the remaining balls, flipping them once with a slotted spoon when the bottom sides are golden brown. You don't want to fry them too fast, as the insides need time to cook.

Drain on paper towels and serve with the fun stuff.

Aegina, Greece

This page: Fish market, Aegina, Greece

Opposite page: Urs Fischer, *Merpig*, 2014

There's as much information out there about which fish to eat or avoid as there are fish in the sea. As it turns out, there are not as many fish in the sea as there used to be, so when thinking about our depleted oceans, here is what I try to do: eat the big guys once in a while and in small quantities; eat the medium guys in good measure; and just eat the small guys whenever you want. And by "guys," I mean fish.

I make fish a few different ways. I most often roast it, I sometimes like to grill or broil it whole, and I rarely sear it. A good wintertime substitute for grilling is to place the fish directly under the broiler. I like this method because it is quick and easy, and in the colder months, there is the illusion of a grilled meal without the inconvenience of actually grilling it.

Fish, like everything else, is best seasoned simply: your arsenal should always include olive oil, salt, and freshly ground black pepper; sometimes lemon juice or oregano; and sometimes both. I serve my fish drizzled with olive oil and garnished with lemon wedges, or with different salads or salsas. I like to pick a fresh seasonal fish and pair it with a salsa that fits the same description. (But not always. What fun is that?)

FISH

"GRILLED" WHOLE FISH, GREEK-STYLE

To me, eating a whole fish with a fork and knife is as sacreligious as eating ribs with a fork and knife—not to mention, it's absolutely wrong and inefficient. Part of the joy in serving a whole fish lies in the tactile sensation of deboning, and in wiping your plate with the remaining morsels to sop up all the lemon and olive oil. By eating with your hands, you can also feel for any stray bones as well as make bad jokes about not knowing how to use proper utensils. I don't like to fill the cavity with anything other than salt, pepper, and oregano. This fish is crispy and delicious out of the oven, without too much fuss.

Per person:

1 whole fish (Porgy, snapper, rainbow trout, and branzino are good choices. Ask your fishmonger to gut and scale the fish for you, keeping the head and tail intact. If the fish is really big, you can get one for two people to share.)
extra-virgin olive oil
salt and freshly ground black pepper
dried oregano
***Latholemono* (page 153)**

If you have a top broiler, place your rack directly under your broiler set on high. Drizzle each fish with olive oil and rub to coat. Sprinkle both sides of each fish with salt, pepper, and oregano. Season the cavity of each fish the same way.

Place the fish in rows on a baking sheet lined with aluminum foil. The fish should be directly under the heat source. Broil until the skin is crisp and bubbly on one side, around 6 to 8 minutes, depending on the size of the fish and the heat from your broiler.

Remove the baking sheet from the oven and wait a minute (I find this helps the fish to unstick) before flipping the fish and returning it to continue broiling on the other side until bubbly and crisp.

To serve:
Let the fish cool slightly. To debone, cut off the head and then remove the spiny dorsal fin on the top. Make a cut down the belly of the fish to the tail. With your fingers (using your hands is by far the easiest technique), gently ease open the fish and remove its spine. Spoon *Latholemono* over the fish.

SEARED TUNA

An old classic that we at the studio like to call "everyman's sashimi," seared tuna lives in the happy place between cooked and raw, giving you the best of both worlds. Make sure you get very fresh and deeply pink tuna steaks to sear and serve with Avocado Salsa (page 152), Apple Fennel Salsa (page 150), or Grape Salsa with Mint (page 150).

Serves 4–6

¼ cup coarsely cracked black pepper
2 fresh tuna steaks about an inch thick (almost 1 pound)
extra-virgin olive oil
salt

Spread the black pepper out on a plate. I usually buy the pepper already coarsely cracked, but you can use a coffee grinder to quickly crack whole peppercorns. Generously sprinkle the tuna with salt on both sides and then press one side of the tuna in the black pepper. (I do only one side because it gets too spicy if you dip both sides in the pepper.) In a pan over high heat, sear the tuna in a drizzle of olive oil. Sear for about 3 minutes on the cracked pepper side, and 2 to 3 minutes on the other side so that the middle is still pink.

Slice the tuna and fan it out on a plate. Serve with the salsa of your choice.

ROASTED SALMON

A side of salmon is perfect for when you're having people over—it looks very extravagant and can be served warm or at room temperature, and everyone has fun helping themselves by breaking off perfectly pink and flaky chunks of fish. This dish pairs well with Apple Fennel Salsa (page 150) and Radish, Watercress, and Basil Salad (page 153).

Serves 8–10

1 side of salmon (around 3 pounds)
extra-virgin olive oil
dried oregano
salt and freshly ground black pepper

Preheat the oven to 400 °F.

Place the side of salmon on a baking sheet and slice 3 or 4 incisions 2 inches apart on the thicker half of the fish, almost as if you are cutting it into serving portions, but stopping halfway from the bottom. Drizzle with a bit of olive oil. Sprinkle generously with salt, pepper, and oregano.

Roast in the oven for 12 to 15 minutes. The salmon should be cooked but still a bit pink in the center. Remember that it will continue to cook after you take it out of the oven.

Serve with the salsa or salad of your choice.

FISH TACOS WITH LIME CREMA

I am not going to try to pretend that any of this is traditional. There are lots of fish taco recipes out there, and this one is mine. I feel that good tacos always pack a punch: Spicy! Lime! Taco time!

I rub the fish with a simple, spicy paste, roast it, and serve it with corn tortillas, crema, spicy salsa, red cabbage, lime wedges, and avocado. You can zip these up further with thinly sliced radishes, jalapeños, and scallions as well. Serve with Fennel Salsa (page 150) or Mango Salsa (page 152).

Serves 6–8

2 pounds of your favorite fish (I like halibut, salmon, or sea bass)
juice of 1 lime
1 tablespoon ground cumin
1 teaspoon dried oregano
¼ teaspoon cayenne pepper
½ teaspoon ground turmeric
extra-virgin olive oil
salt and freshly ground black pepper

Lime Crema:
1 cup sour cream
zest and juice of 1 lime
extra-virgin olive oil
salt and freshly ground black pepper

To serve:
16 corn tortillas
salsa of your choice
a few thinly sliced radishes
shaved red or green cabbage
sliced avocado
thinly sliced jalapeños
chopped scallions
lime wedges

To make the fish:
Preheat the oven to 450 °F.
Whisk the lime juice with the cumin, oregano, cayenne pepper, and turmeric. Add just a bit of olive oil, so the mixture becomes a thick paste. Spread the spice rub on the fish with the back or a spoon, sprinkle with salt and pepper, and roast until just cooked through, about 12 to 14 minutes.

To make the crema:
Whisk the sour cream, lime zest, and juice together. Add a light drizzle of olive oil, season with salt and pepper, and whisk again to combine. Add more lime juice and salt to taste. It should be very tangy.

To serve:
Heat the tortillas up in a dry skillet over high heat, a minute or two per side.
I like to keep things simple and serve the tacos in a "make your own" taco fashion, with a platter of fish, warm tortillas, lime crema, and the fixings all on the side.

WILD STRIPED BASS IN PARCHMENT WITH SWISS CHARD

I am always surprised by just how tasty and refined fish tastes when prepared this way. Everything in this cute little parchment paper pouch is perfectly steamed and infused with flavor, that when topped with a dollop of Quick Lemon Aioli (page 154) really sends you home singing.

Serves 4

4 large leaves Swiss chard, any variety
1 whole lemon
1–1 ½ pounds sea bass, halibut, or any white, fleshy fish, cut into 4 pieces
2 tablespoons cold unsalted butter
4 sprigs of fresh thyme
4 sheets parchment paper, each approximately 1 foot long
extra-virgin olive oil
salt and freshly ground black pepper

Preheat the oven to 400 °F. Wash and dry the chard leaves. Fold each leaf along the stem and cut out the tough stalk.

Slice the lemon into half-moons.

Cube the butter into 4 pieces, one for each piece of fish.

Remove the leaves from the sprigs of thyme and finely chop.

Place a filet of fish at the bottom of a chard leaf, and season it with salt, pepper, and thyme. Top the fish with a slice of lemon and a cube of butter.

Roll up the seasoned fish in the chard leaf and then place the roll in the middle of the parchment sheet. Drizzle the fish bundle with just a bit of olive oil. Bring together of the top and bottom of the parchment paper so that they meet in the middle over the fish and fold down to seal. Fold in the sides to create a little pouch.

Place the parchment packets on a baking pan and roast in the oven for 14 minutes.

Serve in the parchment with Quick Lemon Aioli (page 154) or *Latholemono* (page 153) on the side to spoon over the fish once unwrapped.

SALSAS AND OTHER FIXINGS

APPLE FENNEL SALSA

Tart, crunchy, refreshing, and perfect for the fall or winter, this salsa goes with just about anything.

Makes about 1 ½ cups

1 Granny Smith apple, finely diced
1 fennel bulb, finely diced
juice of 2 limes
1 jalapeño, minced (remove the seeds for less heat)
1 large handful of fresh cilantro, finely chopped
2 scallions, thinly chopped, white and light-green parts only
salt and freshly ground black pepper

Mix all of the ingredients in a bowl and taste for seasoning. If something is missing, it's usually salt or lime juice; add more to taste.

Variations:
Substitute another bulb of fennel for the apple and make it a fennel salsa.
Add 2 teaspoons of toasted and crushed fennel seeds.

GRAPE SALSA WITH MINT

A beautiful and unusual combination, grape salsa is a favorite at the studio in the fall, often gracing the table as an accompaniment to richer fish such as salmon, tuna, or swordfish.

Makes about 1 cup

1 cup seedless red or purple grapes, each sliced into quarters
1 jalapeño, minced (use less for less heat)
juice of 1 lime
1 handful of fresh cilantro, chopped
1 handful of fresh mint, chopped
salt and freshly ground black pepper

Mix all of the ingredients in a bowl and taste for seasoning.

AVOCADO SALSA

The rich flavor and beautiful green color of avocado pairs well with salmon or tuna. Use avocados that are not too ripe; they should just give to gentle pressure.

Makes about 1 cup

2 ripe avocados, diced or thinly sliced
1 handful of fresh cilantro, leaves picked off and left whole
1 jalapeño, thinly sliced
extra-virgin olive oil
juice of 2 limes or 1 lemon
salt and freshly ground black pepper

For this salsa, I don't like to mix all the ingredients together in a bowl because the avocado gets mushy and cloudy. I prefer to slice (or dice) the avocado and place it on the fish, scattering the cilantro leaves and jalapeño slices on top. I then drizzle everything with olive oil and lime or lemon juice, and then season with salt and pepper.

MANGO SALSA

My favorite accompaniment to fish tacos, this salsa is very zesty and tart. Make sure your mangoes are not overripe.

Makes about 1 cup

3 mangoes, peeled and diced
juice of 2 limes
1 jalapeño, minced or grated on a Microplane
1 large handful of fresh cilantro, chopped
salt and freshly ground black pepper

Mix all of the ingredients in a bowl and taste for seasoning.

RADISH, WATERCRESS, AND BASIL SALAD

The basil in this salad is a pleasant surprise, as it blends in with the watercress and stays hidden until you actually take a bite. Lemony and aromatic, this is perfect pairing for salmon.

Makes about 1 cup

1 bunch of radishes, washed and trimmed
1 large bunch of watercress (about 2 cups, thick stems removed)
1 small handful of basil leaves, coarsely torn
extra-virgin olive oil
juice of 1 lemon
salt and freshly ground black pepper

Cut the radishes in half and then slice them into thin half-moons.

Mix the radishes, watercress, and basil in a bowl and drizzle with a bit of olive oil and season with salt and pepper.

Then squeeze the lemon juice over the salad and toss one more time. Taste for seasoning and spoon over fish.

LATHOLEMONO (OLIVE OIL AND LEMON DRESSING)

This classic Greek dressing complements fish perfectly.

Makes about ⅔ cup

⅓ cup extra-virgin olive oil
3 tablespoons fresh lemon juice
1 tablespoon dried oregano
salt and freshly ground black pepper

Whisk the olive oil into the lemon juice with the oregano, a pinch of salt, and a grinding of black pepper. Or even better, shake all of the ingredients in a jar so that they really emulsify.

ALEX'S HOT SAUCE

Alex Eagleton is my best friend, and a hot sauce enthusiast. He makes a versatile red chili sauce that goes with just about anything, but especially with Greek lentil soup (page 75). It is also delicious with Seared Duck Breast (page 160) or plain rice, and is a welcome spicy addition to brothy soups. This hot sauce is not for the faint of heart.

Makes about 2 cups

24 whole garlic cloves, peeled and divided
10 red chili peppers (the long, skinny kind), stems removed
¼ cup granulated sugar
4 tablespoons salt
6 tablespoons rice wine vinegar
⅛ cup water
1 teaspoon ground cumin
3 teaspoons fish sauce
½ teaspoon sesame oil

In a large, dry skillet over medium-high heat, toast 20 of the 24 garlic cloves along with the chili peppers. Flip the cloves and peppers often, so they get browned in spots, about five minutes. Remove from heat.

In a food processor, blend the toasted garlic and chili peppers with the 4 raw garlic cloves, sugar, salt, rice wine vinegar, water, cumin, fish sauce, and sesame oil until smooth.

The sauce will keep in the fridge for about a week.

QUICK LEMON AIOLI

A good aioli should be super-lemony, cutting the richness while still being a lovely creamy addition to fish dishes.

Makes about ½ cup

2 tablespoons fresh lemon juice
zest of 1 lemon
¼ cup mayonnaise
2 tablespoons extra-virgin olive oil
a pinch of salt and freshly ground black pepper

Mix all of the ingredients together in a bowl, adding more lemon juice and another pinch of salt if needed.

Chrisoula and Martha, Elvis Souvlaki, Athens, Greece

Once, for a dinner I was cooking at GBE, I ordered fifty pounds of lamb from an upstate farm to be delivered to my teensy one-bedroom New York City apartment. Fifty pounds of lamb is a lot of meat. It feeds at least 150 people, and does not fit into a normal-size fridge.

I remember my parents were visiting me at the time, sitting quietly on my small couch, horrified at the sight of fifty pounds of lamb, though slightly amused that the farmer who dropped it off tried to exit through the bathroom. And then there was me: Flustered and confused, I had never seen meat in that quantity before. It was my first job cooking for more than a hundred people, and I had to store the rest of the lamb in my neighbor's fridge.

It was the first time I could even slightly wrap my mind around how much meat is consumed in this world, and I finally understood the importance of appreciating our easy access to meat.

Meat is delicious and nourishing. It feels celebratory and opulent. The smell of a braise, and especially a barbecue, sets off the most primal alarm in the brain that sounds something like this: "GOOD! ME WANT!" But make sure to appreciate your meat, and get it from a good and responsible butcher. As my yiayia likes to say, eating meat more than once a week is a modern-day luxury.

MEAT

GREEK-STYLE SEARED SKIRT STEAK WITH LEMON AND OREGANO

This is my American take on how Greeks do meat—grilled; liberally seasoned with salt, black pepper, and oregano; and finished with a squeeze of lemon at serving time. In this version, the steak is marinated in a Greek-inspired emulsion with mustard and garlic added, giving it even more of a juicy kick.

Serves 4

juice of 1 lemon
1 garlic clove, finely chopped
1 tablespoon Dijon mustard
1 teaspoon dried oregano
1 tablespoon extra-virgin olive oil
1 pound skirt steak
salt and freshly ground black pepper

Whisk the lemon juice, garlic, mustard, oregano, and olive oil together in a bowl. Cut the steak into 2 or 3 pieces, place in the bowl, and toss with the marinade. Cover the bowl with plastic wrap and let it sit at room temperature for up to an hour.

Heat a skillet or cast iron pan over medium-high heat until a drop of water sizzles upon contact with the pan. Remove the steak from the marinade, and pat dry. Sprinkle both sides generously with salt and pepper and place the steak in the skillet and don't touch it for 5 minutes.

Flip the steak, and sear for another 5 minutes. Remove the steak from the skillet, and let it rest for at least 10 minutes.

Slice the steak on the diagonal (against the grain of the meat) and serve it on a warmed platter or plate.

Note: Five minutes per side will give you a medium-rare steak, depending on how thick it is. You can sear it for a minute less, or a minute more, depending on how you like it cooked and how thick it is.

SEARED DUCK BREAST WITH ROASTED GRAPES AND SOUR CREAM MUSTARD

Duck breast is pretty fun. The Moulard variety is more tender and less gamy than other varieties, so opt for that if you can find it. The very best part of the duck, of course, is the crispy, salty skin that's essentially wrapped around what tastes like a lean steak. When paired with roasted grapes and sour cream mustard, duck lends itself to a presentation that can't be beat. Kingdoms crumble!

Serves 2

1 Moulard duck breast
salt and freshly ground black pepper

Preheat the oven to 400 °F.
Rinse the duck breast and pat dry.
Score the fatty side of the duck breast in a cross-hatched pattern, without cutting through to the actual meat. This helps the fat render, providing you with that deliciously crisp skin. Season both sides of the breast generously with salt and pepper and set aside.
Heat a heavy, ovenproof skillet over a medium flame and sear the fatty side of the breast first, for about 6 minutes. You will have to drain the pan of the fat once or twice during this time. I do this by pressing down on the breast with one hand, while the other hand tips the pan to pour the fat into a container to save for another use, or discard.
Flip the duck and sear it on the other side for 4 minutes. Both sides should be nice and crispy.
Then stick the entire pan in the oven for 6 or 7 minutes. This will give you a medium-rare duck breast.
Let the duck rest for 10 minutes and then slice on the diagonal, against the grain. Serve with Roasted Purple Grapes and Sour Cream Mustard.

Roasted Purple Grapes

Blistered grapes are delicious served with any gamy meat.

1–2 bunches of seedless purple grapes, left on the vine
extra-virgin olive oil
salt and freshly ground black pepper

Preheat the oven to 400 °F. Drizzle the grapes with olive oil and season them with salt and pepper. Roast for about 25 to 35 minutes; they will be a beautiful deep purple color and bursting with juice.

Sour Cream Mustard

This sauce is not only amazing with the duck; dipping Smashed Crispy Potatoes (page 103) into it is also no joke.

1 tablespoon Dijon mustard
3 tablespoons sour cream
1 tablespoon fresh lemon juice
salt and freshly ground black pepper

Mix all ingredients together and taste for seasoning, adding more lemon juice or mustard as needed. The sauce should be strong and tangy to cut through the richness of the duck and the sweetness of the grapes.

Variations:
To make cherry mustard, omit the sour cream and mix a spoonful of cherry preserves with 2 spoonfuls of Dijon mustard. Apricot preserves are another good option.

SMOKY SPICED CHICKEN KEBABS

I have nothing meaningful or historical to tell you about kebabs. Yes, I'm Greek, and maybe I am genetically predisposed to putting meat on a stick, but the reality is that it tastes good. The marinade soaks into every bite and charred, spiced meat on a stick can't be beat. Chicken is a wonderfully mild meat that happily takes on bold spices and flavors. These kebabs are reminiscent of the NYC street vendors, whose "street meat" fills the air with the smell of something delicious, even if it may not be so "trustworthy." But these kebabs, with *Tah-dig* with Potato Crust (page 127), and Red Cabbage Salad with Pistachios and Mint (page 57)? *YES!*

Serves 4–6

2 pounds boneless, skinless breasts or thigh
salt and freshly ground black pepper
6–10 metal skewers (I prefer metal skewers to wood because they are cheap, you will have them forever, and then you don't have to worry about them breaking or burning.)

Marinade:
juice of 2 lemons
1 tablespoon cumin, seeds or powder
2 teaspoons ground coriander
1 teaspoon ground turmeric
1 teaspoon smoked Spanish-style paprika
1 tablespoon Dijon mustard
2 garlic cloves, finely chopped
1 teaspoon dried oregano
3 tablespoons extra-virgin olive oil

Cut the chicken into 2-inch pieces.
Whisk all of the marinade ingredients together and add the chicken, allow to marinate for up to an hour in the refrigerator. Thread about 4 pieces of chicken on each skewer and sprinkle the kebabs with salt and pepper. Grill the kebabs over medium-hot coals about 5 to 6 minutes per side.

Alternatively, if you have a powerful broiler, prepare a baking sheet by lining it with aluminum foil. Place the skewers in a row on the prepared baking sheet and set an oven rack directly underneath the broiler. Place the chicken in the oven. You want the chicken charred on one side within 5 minutes. Flip the skewers and broil for another 4 to 5 minutes. You can test a skewer by cutting a piece of chicken in half. It should be juicy and cooked all the way through.

Variations:
Lamb kebabs with fennel seeds: *Cube 2 pounds of boneless butterflied leg of lamb into 2-inch pieces and marinate for an hour at room temperature in the same marinade used for the Greek-Style Skirt Steak (page 158), adding 1 tablespoon of fennel seeds. Thread 3 or 4 pieces of lamb onto each skewer, season with salt and freshly ground black pepper, and grill over medium-hot coals for 4 to 5 minutes per side.*

Swordfish kebabs: *Cube 2 pounds of swordfish into 2-inch pieces and marinate for 15 minutes in the same marinade used for the Greek-Style Skirt Steak (page 158). Thread 3 or 4 pieces of swordfish onto each skewer, season with salt and freshly ground black pepper, and grill over medium-hot coals on one side for 5 to 6 minutes; do not flip. The fish should cook through and not stick to the grill if properly charred on one side.*

KOKKINISTO (BRAISED BEEF WITH TOMATOES, CINNAMON, AND CLOVES)

What I love about Greek braises is that they are so simple and delicious. The tomatoes in which the beef are braised give *Kokkinisto* its name, which literally means "red." The cinnamon and cloves always add a sweet and mysterious element that makes people wonder just what is going on in your stew. You can apply this method to chicken and lamb with equally delicious results. In Greece, this dish is served simply with pasta or orzo and a sprinkle of freshly grated cheese. Like all braises, this is best made a day in advance—or do like my yiayia does and make it in the morning to be served for a late lunch.

Serves 4–6

2 pounds beef stew meat, cubed
½ cup red wine (I use anything I don't mind drinking the rest of)
2 yellow onions, finely chopped
2 bay leaves
1 cinnamon stick
3 whole cloves
1 14.5-ounce can of diced or crushed tomatoes
1 fresh tomato, chopped (optional)
salt and freshly ground black pepper
1 small handful of fresh dill, chopped
Parmesan cheese, for serving
pasta or orzo, for serving

Generously salt and pepper the stew meat. Heat the olive oil in a medium heavy-bottomed pot over high heat. Brown the beef on all sides (you will have to do this in batches), and remove it from the pot. Reduce the heat to low, add the wine, and, using a wooden spoon, gently scrape the bottom of the pan.

Add the onions, bay leaves, cinnamon stick, and cloves, and cook over medium-low heat, stirring occasionally until softened and translucent, around 5 minutes.

Add the can of tomatoes and fresh tomato (if using), and then the browned stew meat. Reduce the heat to low and cover the pot.

Simmer for an hour and a half to 2 hours, until the meat is soft and fork-tender.

Taste the sauce and adjust the seasoning, adding a little more salt if necessary. This is better to do when the dish has cooled down a bit so you can really taste the thickened sauce. Garnish with a sprinkle of dill and serve with pasta or orzo and grated Parmesan.

PERSIAN CHICKEN STEW

Warming and aromatic, this stew has a lot in common with the Greek *Kokkinisto* (page 164), but the addition of turmeric, coriander, and cumin takes it in a more exotic direction. Served with Beet Tzatziki (page 25), Saffron Rice (page 122), and a simple green salad with herbs (page 36), you have the makings of a very colorful feast.

Serves 6–8

1 3–3½-pound chicken cut into 10 serving pieces, skin removed (I leave out the wings, but feel free to include them)
1 large yellow onion, finely chopped
extra-virgin olive oil
4 garlic cloves, minced
2 bay leaves
1 cinnamon stick
1 teaspoon ground turmeric
1 teaspoon ground coriander
1 tablespoon ground cumin
½ pound green beans, fresh or frozen, ends trimmed
1 14.5-ounce can of pureed tomatoes
salt and freshly ground black pepper

Season the chicken pieces with salt and pepper and set aside. Sweat the onion with a generous drizzle of olive oil and a generous pinch of salt in a heavy pot over medium heat. Add the garlic and sauté for another 5 minutes until the onions start to soften. Add the bay leaves, cinnamon stick, turmeric, coriander, and cumin to the onion mixture and stir to combine. Cook for 2 minutes to allow the spices to become fragrant. Add the green beans and the tomato puree and bring to a boil. Simmer the beans for 10 minutes and then add the chicken to the pot and with just enough water to come halfway up the chicken. If it doesn't seem like enough water, don't worry—the chicken and beans both release water as they cook. Bring the stew to a simmer, cover with a lid, and cook for 40 to 50 minutes until the chicken and beans are very tender. Allow the stew to cool and taste for seasoning, adding salt and pepper as needed.

This page: Gavin Brown's enterprise, New York

Opposite page: Lamb preparations, The Geffen Contemporary at MOCA, Los Angeles, California

MATT

BRAISED SPICED LAMB WITH YOGURT AND WALNUTS

The combination of the heavily spiced, tender lamb with tangy, cooling yogurt and toasted walnuts is so incredibly good.

Serves 6–8

Spiced Lamb:
2 pounds lamb stew meat, cubed
4 tablespoons all-purpose flour
1 large yellow onion, finely chopped
4 garlic cloves, finely chopped
2 bay leaves
1 tablespoon ground cumin
1 teaspoon ground coriander
1 cinnamon stick
1 teaspoon hot red pepper flakes
2 medium carrots, peeled and sliced on the bias into ¼-inch discs
¾ cup dry red wine or chicken broth
1 28-ounce can of pureed tomatoes
extra-virgin olive oil
salt and freshly ground black pepper

Yogurt Sauce:
2 cups Greek yogurt
1 tablespoon fresh lemon juice
3 tablespoons extra-virgin olive oil
salt and freshly ground black pepper

Garnishes:
1 cup raw walnuts, toasted using Technique #1 (page 34) and chopped
1 handful of fresh flat-leaf parsley, mint, or cilantro leaves, finely chopped

To make the lamb:

Preheat the oven to 350 °F. Generously season the lamb with salt and freshly ground black pepper. Toss the cubes of lamb in the flour, dusting off any excess.

In a heavy pot over medium heat, pour a drizzle of olive oil, just enough to coat the bottom, and sear the lamb in batches. Remove the lamb from the pot and set aside.

Add the onion, garlic, bay leaves, cumin, coriander, cinnamon stick, and pepper flakes to the pot. Add a pinch of salt and a generous grinding of black pepper. Sauté over medium heat until the onion has softened and the spices are fragrant, about 5 minutes.

Add the wine or chicken broth and bring the stew to a boil momentarily, scraping up all the brown bits at the bottom of the pot. Reduce the heat to low and add the lamb, carrots, and tomatoes. Bring the stew to a boil again, and then reduce to a simmer, covering the pot.

Simmer the stew for about an hour to 90 minutes, or alternatively put the stew in a 350 °F oven for 90 minutes, until the meat is fork-tender.

The stew should have a nice thick sauce, but if you'd like to thicken it even more, you can whisk a ladleful of broth with 2 tablespoons of flour and add it back to the stew, simmering until it thickens up a bit. If you find the sauce is too thick, you can thin it out with a bit of water or broth.

To make the yogurt sauce:

While the stew is cooking, mix the yogurt with the lemon juice and olive oil, and season with salt and freshly ground black pepper.

To serve, spread the yogurt on a platter, using the back of a spoon to push it to the edges and create a well in the center. Ladle the stew in the middle and garnish generously with chopped walnuts and your herb of choice.

Yiayia's centerpiece, Aegina, Greece

This page: Plums at the Union Square Greenmarket, New York
Opposite page: Peter Regli, *thank you mina stone*, 2014

I tend to put people into two categories: those who eat dessert and those who don't. People often protest that they are "too full" to eat dessert, and here's what I say to that: Dessert is not about hunger; therefore, you can't be too full to eat dessert. Dessert symbolically closes the meal. It is one last hurrah, a final gesture of generosity and abundance. I like dessert to be rich and yummy, but not too sweet or over-the-top heavy. I use lots of Greek yogurt in my desserts because it encompasses those balanced qualities and is a great platform for fruit compotes. In all of my recipes, the sugar measurement is about half what it could be. If you have a sweeter tooth, increase the sugar.

SWEET THINGS

PEARS WITH LEMON, CINNAMON, AND HONEY

I had this dessert at a seaside taverna one fall, and have been making it ever since. The lemon and honey give the pears a naturally sweet-and-sour taste that is perfectly complemented by the spicy cinnamon.

Serves 6–8

4 just ripe pears, your favorite type (Anjou is mine)
juice of 1 lemon
honey (preferably Greek thyme honey)
1 teaspoon ground cinnamon

Slice each pear into 8 wedges, removing the core. Drizzle the fruit with the lemon juice and honey, sprinkle with the cinnamon, and serve.

***Variation:** Substitute apples for the pears.*

GREEK YOGURT PANNA COTTA WITH MASTIC AND APRICOT COMPOTE

Mastiha (mastic) is one of my favorite flavors. It is the resin from the mastic tree that only grows on the island of Chios and has been used in Greece in cooking and for its medicinal properties since ancient times. It imparts a distinct pine taste to desserts that is indescribable and exotic. Mastic is available at Greek and Middle Eastern grocery stores, but if you can't find it, you can leave it out.

Serves 8

Panna Cotta:
2 tablespoons water
2 tablespoons fresh lemon juice
2 ½ teaspoons unflavored gelatin
2 ¼ cups whole-milk Greek yogurt
1 ¾ heavy cream, divided
¾ cup granulated sugar
½ teaspoon ground mastic
vegetable oil, for greasing

Apricot Compote:
15 fresh apricots, halved with pits removed
2 tablespoons granulated sugar
1 tablespoon water
2 teaspoons fresh lemon juice
1 teaspoon pure vanilla extract

To make the panna cotta:
Lightly oil eight 4-ounce ramekins. (I like using little glasses or bowls too.)
Combine the water and lemon juice in a small bowl. Sprinkle the gelatin on top and whisk to combine. Allow the gelatin mixture to soften for about 15 minutes.
In a large bowl whisk the yogurt and ¾ cup of the heavy cream and set aside.
In a saucepan, combine the remaining 1 cup of heavy cream with the sugar and bring to a simmer over medium heat, stirring until the sugar dissolves.
Remove from heat and add the gelatin mixture, whisking until the gelatin dissolves.
Add the mastic, and whisk again.
Add the gelatin/cream mixture to the yogurt mixture and whisk together.
Pour into the prepared ramekins, allow to cool a bit, and then cover with plastic wrap. Refrigerate until cold, at least 3 to 4 hours.

To make the compote:
In a medium saucepan over medium-low heat, place the apricots, sugar, lemon juice, water, and vanilla extract. Simmer until the apricots are very soft and falling apart, about 20 minutes. You can mash the apricots with the bottom of a glass to get a chunky consistency. Allow the compote to cool and thicken, and serve spooned over the cold panna cotta.

Variations:
You can make this compote with any fresh fruit in season or even frozen fruit. A jammy compote like this is also delicious with plain yogurt.

MAPLE YOGURT WITH BERRY COMPOTE

This simple dessert has a kind of loveliness that is difficult to describe: the yogurt and fruit are perfectly balanced in sweetness, tartness, and creaminess. This is a dessert I have served over and over again, switching the compote to any sort of fruit I feel like. I find that berries, especially strawberries, never go out of style.

Serves 6

Maple Yogurt:
⅓ cup pure maple syrup
2 cups whole-milk or 2% Greek yogurt

Berry Compote:
1 pound strawberries, hulled and cut in half
1 cup blueberries, blackberries, raspberries, or a mix
1 teaspoon pure vanilla extract
2 teaspoons fresh lemon juice
2 tablespoons granulated sugar

To make the maple yogurt:
Whisk the maple syrup into the yogurt and set aside.

To make the compote:
Simmer the berries, vanilla extract, lemon juice, and sugar in a saucepan over medium-low heat until the berries are soft and falling apart, about 15 minutes. Let the berry compote cool, and then alternate layers of fruit and yogurt in 6 small clear glasses (or dessert bowls), finishing with the berry compote.

Make ahead: The yogurt and the compote can be made and stored in the fridge up to 2 days in advance.

Variations:
Use whatever seasonal fruit you have on hand to make the compote. Stone fruits such as cherries, plums, and peaches are a great option.

MILK CHOCOLATE PUDDING WITH VANILLA CREAM

I have always been a fan of milk chocolate more than dark, and this pudding is the perfect way to showcase its virtues. It's a creamy, chocolate-y goodness that is not too sweet, and very difficult to stop eating. I like to call the topping vanilla cream instead of whipped cream because it gives a better understanding of what the consistency should be like—more like almost melted ice cream rather than traditional whipped cream.

Serves 6

Chocolate Pudding:
2 tablespoons granulated sugar
2 tablespoons cornstarch
2 tablespoons unsweetened cocoa powder
⅛ teaspoon salt
1 ½ cups whole milk
½ cup heavy cream
8 ounces fine-quality milk chocolate, broken into pieces
1 teaspoon pure vanilla extract

Vanilla Cream:
1 pint heavy cream
1 tablespoon granulated sugar
1 vanilla bean

To make the chocolate pudding:
In a heavy saucepan whisk together the sugar, cornstarch, cocoa powder, and salt. Turn the heat on to medium-high and gradually whisk in the milk and cream and bring to a boil. Make sure you are whisking the entire time. Once the mixture has thickened, whisk in the chocolate and vanilla extract and remove the pudding from the heat.
Transfer the pudding to a bowl and cover the surface with plastic wrap to prevent a skin from forming. Chill for about 2 hours.

To make the vanilla cream:
Pour the heavy cream into a bowl and add the sugar. Slice the vanilla bean down the middle and scrape the seeds into the cream. You can swirl the bean around in the cream to get all the seeds out. Discard the bean. Using an electric mixer, whip the cream until soft peaks form.

Spoon the pudding into 6 bowls and top each bowl with a spoonful of the vanilla cream.

Make ahead: The pudding can be made 2 days in advance.

Variations:
Use dark chocolate instead of milk chocolate if you prefer the taste, or use a combination of both.
Serve the pudding with sliced banana on top and then add the vanilla cream.

STRAWBERRY RHUBARB CRUMBLE

My favorite part of a crumble is the crumble itself. Let's be honest—it is the best part. I like to make crumbles with double the topping so that everyone is sure to get lots of the good stuff in their serving. Strawberry rhubarb is my favorite springtime combination, but use any seasonal fruit you like.

Serves 8

Fruit Filling:
3 pounds fresh strawberries, hulled and cut in half
1 cup fresh rhubarb, cut into ¼-inch dice
¼ cup granulated sugar
1 tablespoon fresh lemon juice
1 teaspoon pure vanilla extract

Crumble:
1 ½ cups all-purpose flour
¾ cup granulated sugar
½ teaspoon salt
zest of 1 orange
¼ teaspoon ground nutmeg
10 tablespoons unsalted butter, chilled and cut into small cubes
2 cups old-fashioned oats
1 ½ cup raw pecans, coarsely chopped

vanilla ice cream or whipped cream, for serving

To make the fruit filling:
Preheat the oven to 375 °F. Butter a 12 x 8–inch baking dish, or something equivalent in size.
Toss the fruit in a large bowl with the sugar, lemon juice, and vanilla extract. Let the fruit macerate while you make the topping.

To make the crumble:
In a food processor, pulse the flour, sugar, salt, orange zest, nutmeg, and butter until the butter is cut into the flour. It should be only very slightly crumbly, with pea-sized pieces of butter. Stir in the oats and chopped pecans.

Place the fruit filling in the baking dish and top with the crumble mixture. Bake for 40 to 45 minutes, until the crumble is just light brown in spots.

Serve with vanilla ice cream or barely sweetened whipped cream.

PLUM AND GREEK YOGURT TIRAMISU

I first made this one summer when I had a bounty of fresh plums that I cooked into batches of deep purple compote. Brainstorming ways to use it, I replaced the traditional lady finger soak in espresso with the juice from the compote, and some of the mascarpone with Greek yogurt, and out came this fresh and colorful version of tiramisu.

Serves 8–10

Plum Compote:
3 pounds plums, quartered and pitted (after cutting them, they should measure roughly 3 cups)
½ cup granulated sugar
1 tablespoon balsamic vinegar
1 cinnamon stick

Cream Base:
10 ounces mascarpone
1 cup 2% Greek yogurt
¼ cup heavy cream
¼ cup granulated sugar
1 teaspoon pure vanilla extract
1 teaspoon ground cinnamon

1 7-ounce package Italian lady fingers

To make the plum compote:
Place the fruit, sugar, vinegar, and cinnamon stick in a medium heavy pot and simmer over medium-low heat for about 20 minutes, until the plums have softened and turned a bright purple color—don't worry if it seems like there isn't enough liquid, because the fruit will release its juices. Set the plum compote aside. When cooled down from hot to warm, strain the compote and save the plum syrup.

To make the cream base:
Whisk the mascarpone, yogurt, cream, sugar, vanilla extract, and cinnamon together so that everything is well incorporated. Taste and add more sugar if you would like—this dessert shouldn't be too sweet. Set aside.
Mix the strained plums back into the rest of the compote and keep the cup of plum syrup separate.
Dip the lady fingers into the plum syrup and then place them in a single layer in the bottom of a round 9-inch springform cake pan. Some won't fit in the edges, so just cut them in half or smaller to fill the entire bottom. Spoon a generous layer of plum compote on top of the lady fingers and then spoon half the cream base over them. Add a second layer of dipped lady fingers on top of the cream. Spoon a little more compote on top of them and finish with the rest of the cream.
Cover with plastic, and chill the tiramisu for 6 hours or overnight.

To serve:
Remove the tiramisu from the refrigerator 15 minutes before serving. Run a knife around the ring of the pan to release the tiramisu. Slice and serve as is, or with more plum compote spooned on top.

OLIVE OIL CAKE

Ah, olive oil cake. It is the only reason why my friends are friends with me, and why new people start to like me. This recipe creates a cake that is dense, orangey, and spicy with cinnamon and cloves. It is not light on the olive oil and that is really the way it should be.

Serves 10–12

3 large eggs
1 ½ cups extra-virgin olive oil
1 ¼ cups granulated sugar, plus a tablespoon to sprinkle on top
1 ¼ cup milk
¼ cup cognac (optional)
¼ cup fresh orange juice
zest of 1 orange
2 cups all-purpose flour
½ teaspoon baking soda
½ teaspoon baking powder
2 teaspoons ground cinnamon
½ teaspoon ground cloves
1 teaspoon salt

Preheat the oven to 350 °F. Lightly oil a 10-inch round cake pan and dust it with flour.

Whisk the eggs with the olive oil in a bowl until combined. Add the sugar and whisk well to incorporate. Add the milk, cognac (if using), orange juice, and orange zest and whisk again.

In a separate large bowl, mix the other dry ingredients (flour, baking soda, baking powder, cinnamon, cloves, and salt), and make a well in the center.

Pour the olive oil mixture into the dry ingredients, and whisk, starting from the center and working outward, until the batter is smooth.

Pour the batter into the prepared pan and sprinkle another tablespoon of sugar on top. Bake for 50 to 60 minutes. The cake is ready when the top is crusty and dark brown and a skewer or knife inserted in the center comes out clean.

Variations:

After the cake has cooled, dust the top with confectioners' sugar and cinnamon.

Add 1 cup toasted and chopped walnuts to the batter for a nutty taste and texture.

BANANA BREAD WITH WALNUTS AND DARK CHOCOLATE

Banana bread is not an everyday treat in Greece, so when I make this for family and friends, I take extra care to make it the best banana bread possible. Including lots of extra bananas, dark chocolate, and walnuts makes every piece a mosaic of flavor.

Makes one loaf

1 ½ cups all-purpose flour
1 teaspoon baking soda
1 teaspoon baking powder
¼ teaspoon salt
½ cup granulated or brown sugar
½ cup unsalted butter (1 stick), at room temperature
3 large overripe bananas, peeled
2 large eggs
1 teaspoon pure vanilla extract
1 tablespoon fresh lemon juice
½ cup or more bittersweet chocolate, cut into small pieces
½ cup raw walnuts, chopped

Preheat the oven to 350 °F. Butter a loaf pan or a 9-inch round cake pan.

Whisk the flour, baking soda, baking powder, and salt together in a bowl.

In a separate bowl, whisk the sugar with the butter until light and fluffy.

In another bowl, mash the bananas using your hands or the bottom of a glass. Add the eggs to the bananas and whisk. Add the vanilla extract and lemon juice and whisk again.

Add the banana mixture to the sugar mixture and whisk well. Whisk in the flour, and then fold in the chocolate and walnuts.

Spread the batter in the prepared pan and bake for about 45 minutes, until golden on the top and around the edges, and a skewer or knife inserted into the middle comes out clean.

Variations:

This is a great recipe for all different kinds of flours. Rice, amaranth, and oat flour all work very well. My favorite combo is 1 cup oat flour, 1/4 cup brown rice flour, and 1/4 cup amaranth flour. I find that too much rice flour can make baked goods gritty, so go easy on that one.

PISTACHIO ORANGE FLOWER COOKIES

These cookies are based on a Greek Christmas cookie called *kourambiedes*, which are traditionally made with walnuts. They are the most epic butter cookies, falling apart and melting in your mouth the second you take a bite. I like to substitute pistachios for the walnuts as they lend a pretty pale green color to the cookies and as a nod to Aegina, an island famous for its pistachios.

Makes about 2 dozen

¾ cup raw pistachios
1½ cups all-purpose flour
½ teaspoon baking powder
¼ teaspoon salt
½ cup (1 stick) unsalted butter, at room temperature
⅓ cup confectioners' sugar, plus more for rolling
1 large egg yolk
1 tablespoon brandy or cognac
1 teaspoon pure vanilla extract
2 tablespoons orange flower water

Prepare two baking sheets lined with parchment paper.
Pulse the pistachios in a food processor until they have the consistency of breadcrumbs. It is okay if there are some larger pieces as well. Remove to a bowl and mix the pistachios with the flour, baking powder, and salt.
In a large bowl, using an electric mixer (or a whisk and a strong wrist), beat the butter with ⅓ cup of the confectioners' sugar.
Add the egg yolk and beat until incorporated. Add the brandy or cognac and the vanilla extract.
Add the pistachio/flour mixture to the bowl, a bit at a time, and beat on low speed until the dough just comes together. Do not overmix. The dough will be very crumbly and will not completely stick together.
Cover the dough with plastic wrap and let it rest for an hour.

Preheat the oven to 350 °F. Using a tablespoon as a mold, pack the dough into the spoon, and then gently slide the dough off so that the top is a dome and the bottom is flat.
Bake the cookies for 15 to 18 minutes, until the bottoms are golden brown and the cookies are fragrant.
When you take the cookies out of the oven, have the orange flower water ready in a small bowl. Dip your fingers into the water, and flick your fingers over the hot cookies so you hear it sizzle and steam. You will likely not use all of the orange blossom water—just a bit goes a long way.
Roll the warm cookies in confectioners' sugar and place on a pretty platter.

Make ahead: These cookies keep well in an airtight container for at least a couple of weeks.

Variations:
Use toasted walnuts or almonds in place of the pistachios.

BAKLAVA

Homemade baklava is the best. This honey-soaked, buttery, cinnamony, and walnuty version is the real deal. I like to shape my baklava in spirals, like my yiayia taught me, so you can see the filling in each piece. I use very little sugar in the filling as I find that the honey syrup is sweet enough. Don't let phyllo dough intimidate you! It's not that hard, I promise.

Makes about 40 pieces

Baklava:
¼ cup granulated sugar
1 ½ teaspoons ground cinnamon
½ teaspoon ground cloves
2 cups raw walnuts
2 cups raw almonds
1 cup (2 sticks) unsalted butter
1-pound package phyllo, thawed (follow manufacturer's directions)

Honey Syrup:
1 cup honey (preferably Greek thyme honey)
2 cups water
1 cinnamon stick
1 tablespoon fresh lemon juice

To make the baklava:
Preheat the oven to 350 °F. Butter a baking sheet.
Pulse the sugar, cinnamon, cloves, walnuts, and almonds in a food processor until they resemble coarse breadcrumbs. Alternatively, finely chop the nuts and mix them with the sugar and spices. Set the nut mixture aside.
Melt the butter in a saucepan over low heat and then skim the white froth and milk solids that rise to the surface of the liquefied butter. This is now clarified butter. Set aside.
Unroll the phyllo and place one sheet in front of you, oriented vertically. Brush it with the clarified butter using a pastry brush or the back of a spoon, and then place another sheet on top and butter it, repeating to create a stack of 4 layers of buttered phyllo.
Spread about 8 tablespoons of the nut mixture in an even, thin layer over the phyllo stack.
Roll the nut-covered phyllo into a log from top to bottom and cut it into 1½-inch pieces—you should get about 8 pieces of baklava from each roll. Place the pieces spiral-side up on the prepared baking sheet, leaving just a little bit of space between each baklava.
Repeat with the remaining phyllo and spoon any remaining nut mixture or melted butter over the tops of the sliced baklava.
Bake for about 40 minutes until golden brown. Prepare the honey syrup while the baklava bakes.

To make the honey syrup:
Combine the honey, water, and cinnamon stick in a saucepan and bring to a boil. Reduce the heat and simmer until the syrup has slightly thickened, about 10 minutes. Remove from the heat and add the lemon juice. Let the syrup cool to room temperature.
Pour the syrup over the hot baklava when it comes out of the oven. The baklava will sizzle a bit as you pour the syrup over it. There should be a modest pool of syrup that the baklava sits in. Serve at room temperature.

Make ahead: The baklava will keep for 3 to 4 days covered and at room temperature.

This spread: Sunset, ferry from Aegina to Piraeus, Greece

Previous spread: Spencer Sweeney, *Dinner*, 2014

METRIC CONVERSIONS

STARTERS

VEGETABLES WITH LEMON JUICE AND SALT (page 19)

cucumbers, radishes, or carrots
fresh lemon juice
salt
fresh mint leaves, flat-leaf parsley leaves, and/or thinly sliced jalapeños (optional)

KOPANISTI (WHIPPED FETA) (page 20)

Serves 6–8

100 g Greek or French feta
60 g whole-milk ricotta
a pinch of hot red pepper flakes (add more to make it spicier)
a pinch of dried oregano
80 mL extra-virgin olive oil, plus more for drizzling

ELIES TSAKISTES (OLIVES WITH CORIANDER SEEDS AND LEMON PEEL) (page 22)

20 g whole coriander seeds
150 g Castelvetrano or Picholine olives
1 garlic clove, peeled and sliced in thirds (optional)
2 slices of lemon peel
a few fresh rosemary leaves
extra-virgin olive oil

BEET TZATZIKI WITH WALNUTS AND MINT (page 25)

Serves 6–8

2 medium red beets
500 g whole-milk Greek yogurt
1 or 2 garlic cloves (depending on your preference), finely minced
70 g raw walnuts, toasted using Technique #1 (page 34) and finely chopped
30 mL fresh lemon juice
50 mL extra-virgin olive oil
1 handful of fresh mint leaves, finely chopped; reserve a pinch for garnish
salt and freshly ground black pepper

SALADS

FRESH LEMON JUICE DRESSING (page 33)

50 mL fresh lemon juice
150 mL extra-virgin olive oil
salt and freshly ground black pepper
finely chopped shallots and/or a spoonful of good mustard (optional)

TANGY SOUR CREAM DRESSING (page 33)

50 mL fresh lemon juice
100 g sour cream
50 mL extra-virgin olive oil
salt and freshly ground black pepper

GREEN GODDESS SPIN-OFF (page 33)

50 mL fresh lemon juice
100 g sour cream or buttermilk
50 mL extra-virgin olive oil
25 g combination of herbs: parsley, tarragon, mint and/or cilantro
salt and freshly ground black pepper

TAHINI DRESSING (page 33)

scant 50 mL fresh lemon juice
100 g tahini
50 g extra-virgin olive oil
salt and freshly ground black pepper

PRASINI SALATA (GREEN SALAD) (page 36)

Serves 6–8

1 head of romaine lettuce, outer leaves removed
2 handfuls of fresh dill, chopped
3 scallions, finely chopped
extra-virgin olive oil
juice of 1 lemon
salt and freshly ground black pepper

TARTINES WITH PARMESAN, HONEY, AND THYME (page 26)

Serves 8–10

1 baguette, sliced into ½-cm diagonal pieces
extra-virgin olive oil or unsalted butter
50 g Parmesan cheese, thinly sliced with a mandoline or vegetable peeler
honey
8 g fresh thyme leaves
freshly ground black pepper

Cooking temperature: 200 °C

EARLY SPRING SALAD (page 38)
Serves 6

400 g of salad greens of your choice (red romaine leaves, red butter lettuce, arugula, baby chard, or baby kale leaves)
1 handful of fresh mint leaves, roughly torn
3–4 stalks of asparagus, cut as thinly as possible on the bias
2 handfuls of snap peas, cut on the bias
3–4 radishes, thinly sliced
50 g good-quality Pecorino, shaved into ribbons with a vegetable peeler
Fresh Lemon Juice Dressing or Tangy Sour Cream Dressing (page 33)
salt and freshly ground black pepper

HERB SALAD WITH FETA AND TOASTED ALMONDS (page 41)
Serves 4

2 bunches of fresh flat-leaf parsley
1 bunch of fresh mint
1 bunch of fresh cilantro
1 small handful of fresh tarragon leaves
Fresh Lemon Juice Dressing (page 33)
100 g raw sliced almonds, toasted using Technique #1 (page 34)
200 g Greek or French feta, crumbled

HEIRLOOM TOMATOES WITH FETA AND MINT (page 42)
Serves 8

4 large heirloom tomatoes
extra-virgin olive oil
200 g French or Greek feta, crumbled
1 small handful of fresh mint, chopped
1 large handful of micro greens or purslane, leaves only
50 g Kalamata or Picholine olives, pitted and coarsely chopped
salt and fresh ground black pepper

GRATED BEET, CARROT, RADISH, AND AVOCADO SALAD WITH TAHINI DRESSING (page 46)
Serves 8–10

4 carrots, peeled and grated
1 daikon radish, peeled and grated
1 watermelon radish, grated (substitute a second daikon if you can't find a watermelon radish)
2 medium red beets, peeled and grated
Tahini Dressing (page 33)
fresh lemon juice
2 ripe avocados
salt and freshly ground black pepper

RAW CORN SALAD WITH TOASTED ALMONDS AND LIME (page 49)
Serves 4–6

5 ears of corn, shucked and washed
1 fresh jalapeño, finely chopped (optional)
2 large handfuls of flat-leaf parsley, chopped
100 g whole raw almonds, toasted using Technique #1 (page 34) and coarsely chopped
extra-virgin olive oil
juice of 2 limes
salt and freshly ground black pepper

CABBAGE SALAD WITH APPLES, PUMPKIN SEEDS, AND AVOCADO (page 50)
Serves 6–8

1 medium head of red or green cabbage, very thinly sliced
1 tart apple (such as Granny Smith or Pink Lady), diced
2 large handfuls of flat-leaf parsley, coarsely chopped
80 g raw pumpkin seeds, toasted using Technique #2 (page 34)
1 avocado, sliced
Fresh Lemon Juice Dressing or Tangy Sour Cream Dressing (page 33)
1 handful of micro greens (pretty, but totally unnecessary if you don't have them)
salt and freshly ground black pepper

SOUPS

SHAVED BRUSSELS SPROUTS WITH PARMESAN AND ALMONDS (page 52)

Serves 6–8

1 kg brussels sprouts, ends trimmed and outer leaves removed
120 g freshly grated Parmesan cheese
220 g slivered or sliced almonds,
toasted using Technique #1 (page 34)
Fresh Lemon Juice Dressing (page 33)
extra-virgin olive oil

SHAVED CAULIFLOWER WITH PINE NUTS, CURRANTS, AND PARSLEY (page 55)

Serves 6–8

1 small to medium head of cauliflower
100 g raw pine nuts, toasted using Technique #2 (page 34)
50 g black currants
1 handful of flat-leaf parsley leaves, coarsely chopped
Fresh Lemon Juice Dressing (page 33)
salt and freshly ground black pepper

RED CABBAGE, PISTACHIO, AND MINT (page 56)

Serves 8

1 medium head of red cabbage, outer leaves removed
200 g raw pistachios, toasted using Technique #2 (page 34)
and finely chopped
1 large handful of fresh mint leaves, finely chopped
extra-virgin olive oil
juice of 2 lemons
salt and freshly ground black pepper

GREEK FRIED EGGS (page 60)

Per person:

2 eggs
extra-virgin olive oil
salt and freshly ground black pepper

KOTOSOUPA (GREEK CHICKEN SOUP WITH LEMON) (page 66)

Serves 6–8

Broth:
1 whole chicken (1–1.5 kg) cut into 8 pieces
2 yellow onions, peeled and left whole
4 heads of garlic (leave the heads whole, or in pieces with
the peel on, but cut off the root bottoms)
2 bay leaves
15 g whole black peppercorns
12 g kosher salt

Soup:
1 of the cooked chicken breasts from the broth, shredded
(or add more, if you'd like)
1 medium potato (any variety), peeled and diced
juice of 2 lemons
2 large eggs, beaten well
freshly ground black pepper
hot red pepper flakes
lemon wedges, for serving

SPANISH-STYLE GAZPACHO (page 69)

Serves 4–6

8 ripe red tomatoes, beefsteak or heirloom variety
2 large seedless cucumbers, peeled
1 red or green bell pepper
¼ small red onion
1 garlic clove
2 slices of stale rustic bread, soaked in water for a minute (optional)
100 mL extra-virgin olive oil, plus more for serving
40 mL balsamic vinegar
50 mL water
salt and freshly ground black pepper
ice cubes, for serving

ROOT VEGETABLE SOUP WITH PISTACHIO PARSLEY PESTO (page 70)

Serves 6–8

Root Vegetable Soup:
2 yellow onions, diced
4 garlic cloves, coarsely chopped
1 small butternut squash, peeled, seeded, and diced
1 sweet potato, peeled and diced
1 potato, peeled and diced
2 carrots, diced
4 whole sprigs of fresh thyme
2 bay leaves
2 strips of orange peel
extra-virgin olive oil
2 red beets, peeled and diced (optional)
salt and freshly ground black pepper

Pistachio Parsley Pesto:
25 g fresh flat-leaf parsley leaves
40 g raw pistachios, shelled
zest of 1 lemon
1 garlic clove (optional)
50 mL fresh lemon juice
80 mL extra-virgin olive oil
salt and freshly ground black pepper

RED LENTIL SOUP WITH CUMIN AND LIME (page 72)

Serves 6–8

500 g red lentils
15 g unsalted butter
1 yellow onion, coarsely chopped
2 garlic cloves, coarsely chopped
1 bay leaf
5 g cumin seeds
3 g ground turmeric
1 jalapeño, coarsely chopped (optional)
extra-virgin olive oil
2 handfuls of fresh cilantro, finely chopped
salt and freshly ground black pepper
lime wedges, for serving

FAKI (GREEK LENTIL SOUP WITH CINNAMON AND CLOVES) (page 75)

Serves 6–8

1 large yellow onion, finely chopped
3 garlic cloves, finely chopped
500 g green or black lentils, rinsed
2 whole bay leaves
1 cinnamon stick
2 whole cloves
3 g hot red pepper flakes
80 mL extra-virgin olive oil
400 g diced or pureed tomatoes
salt and freshly ground black pepper
30–45 mL red wine vinegar (optional)

REVITHIA (CHICKPEA STEW WITH ROSEMARY, LEMON, AND OLIVE OIL) (page 76)

Serves 6

500 g dried (not canned) chickpeas
15 g baking soda
2 yellow onions, peeled and left whole
2 bay leaves
2 sprigs of fresh rosemary
40 g all-purpose flour
80 mL extra-virgin olive oil
juice of 1–2 lemons
salt and freshly ground black pepper

SPICY CHICKPEA STEW (page 80)

Serves 8–10

500 g dried chickpeas
15 g baking soda
1 large yellow onion, finely chopped
2 garlic cloves, finely chopped
1 jalapeño or serrano pepper, finely chopped
2 bay leaves
15 g cumin seeds
5 g ground coriander
5 g hot red pepper flakes
2 handfuls of fresh flat-leaf parsley, chopped, plus more for serving
400 g diced tomatoes
extra-virgin olive oil
salt and freshly ground black pepper
Greek yogurt, for serving

VEGETABLES

AGINARES ME ARAKA (BRAISED ARTICHOKES, PEAS, AND POTATOES IN LEMON AND OLIVE OIL) (page 88)

Serves 4–6

juice of 2 lemons (or more, to taste)
6 artichoke hearts, fresh or frozen
extra-virgin olive oil
1 bunch of scallions, chopped, white and light-green parts only
2 handfuls of fresh dill, chopped
2 medium waxy potatoes, each cut into 8 chunks
250 g peas, fresh or frozen
6 g all-purpose flour
salt and freshly ground black pepper

FASOLAKIA (BRAISED GREEN BEANS IN TOMATO AND OLIVE OIL) (page 91)

Serves 4–6

1 large yellow onion, chopped
extra-virgin olive oil
500 g green beans, ends trimmed
1 bay leaf
400 g crushed tomatoes or 4 fresh tomatoes, grated
salt and freshly ground black pepper

GRILLED RAMPS WITH CRUSHED HAZELNUTS AND LEMON (page 92)

Serves 4–6

500 g ramps, ends cut off and washed well (they tend to be very dirty things)
extra-virgin olive oil
100 g raw hazelnuts, toasted using Technique #1 (page 34) and finely chopped
juice of 1 lemon
salt and freshly ground black pepper

ROASTED ACORN SQUASH WITH THYME (page 94)

Serves 6–8

3 acorn squashes, washed, halved and seeds scraped out
extra-virgin olive oil
4 or 5 sprigs of fresh thyme
salt and freshly ground black pepper

Cooking temperature: 200 °C

ROASTED CAULIFLOWER AND CAULIFLOWER LEAVES WITH SPICES (page 97)

Serves 4

1 head of cauliflower
extra-virgin olive oil
a sprinkle of hot red pepper flakes
a sprinkle of fennel seeds
a generous sprinkle of cumin seeds
salt and freshly ground black pepper
1 handful of fresh flat-leaf parsley (optional)

Cooking temperature: 200 °C

ROASTED FETA, PEPPERS, AND TOMATOES (page 98)

Serves 4–6

6 Anaheim peppers
a hunk of French or Greek feta (about 150 g, crumbled)
2 ripe tomatoes, coarsely chopped
extra-virgin olive oil
a generous pinch of dried oregano
salt and freshly ground black pepper

Cooking temperature: 220 °C

PASTA

ROASTED CARROTS WITH AVOCADO, CILANTRO, AND LIME (page 100)

Serves 4–6

8–10 large carrots, scrubbed well (peeled if very dirty) and sliced on the diagonal 1 cm thick
extra-virgin olive oil
a generous sprinkle of ground cumin (you want a light dusting on every carrot)
a generous sprinkle of fennel seeds
a sprinkle of hot red pepper flakes
1–2 ripe avocados, sliced
juice of 1 lime
1 handful of fresh cilantro leaves
salt and freshly ground black pepper
1 handful of arugula or other pretty greens (optional)

Cooking temperature: 200 °C

SMASHED CRISPY POTATOES (page 103)

Serves 4–6

1 kg small “new” potatoes, red-skinned or yellow-skinned (think 3–4 potatoes per person)
extra-virgin olive oil
2 sprigs of fresh rosemary
a pinch of dried oregano
salt and freshly ground black pepper

Cooking temperature: the highest setting on your broiler, or 220 °C

BEET FRITTERS (page 105)

Makes 18–20

500 g red beets, scrubbed clean and coarsely grated (about 3–4 medium beets)
1 large russet potato, peeled and coarsely grated
1 large egg
50 g all-purpose flour
2 handfuls of fresh mint, chopped
salt and freshly ground black pepper
frying oil (safflower, canola, and vegetable oil all work well)

MAKARONIA ME KIMA (CINNAMON AND CLOVE MEAT RAGÙ) (page 110)

Serves 4

1 medium yellow onion, finely chopped
extra-virgin olive oil
1 cinnamon stick
3 whole cloves
a pinch of hot red pepper flakes
500 g ground beef
400 g can of pureed tomatoes
500 g pasta of your choice
1 bay leaf
salt and freshly ground black pepper
Parmesan cheese, for serving

EGG NOODLES WITH GARLIC, CHILI, LEMON ZEST, AND PARSLEY (page 113)

Serves 4–6

3 or 4 garlic cloves, finely chopped
extra-virgin olive oil
2–4 g hot red pepper flakes, depending on how spicy you like it
zest of 1 lemon
500 g Greek egg noodles
1 bunch of fresh flat-leaf parsley, finely chopped
salt and freshly ground black pepper
Kefalograviera or Parmesan cheese, grated (optional)

ORZO WITH BLACK PEPPER, PINE NUTS, AND BUTTER (page 114)

Serves 4–6

500 g orzo
50 g unsalted butter
extra-virgin olive oil
25 g freshly ground black pepper
100 g Parmesan cheese, freshly grated (or more, to taste)
50 g raw pine nuts, toasted using Technique #2 (page 34)
salt

GRAINS AND PULSES

SAFFRON RICE (page 122)

Serves 6

400 g basmati rice, rinsed in cold water at least 5 times, until the water starts to run clear
50 g unsalted butter
salt
2 bay leaves
2 pinches of saffron threads

TAH-DIG WITH PISTACHIOS, APRICOTS, AND CARAMELIZED ONIONS (page 124)

Serves 4–6

50 g unsalted butter, plus more as necessary
1 small yellow onion, chopped
100 g dried apricots, cut into slivers
110 g raw pistachios, shelled, toasted using Technique #2 (page 34), and chopped
400 g long-grain rice (such as basmati or jasmine)
15–30 mL extra-virgin olive oil
150 mL hot water
salt

TAH-DIG WITH POTATO CRUST (page 127)

Serves 6

400 g long-grain rice (such as basmati or jasmine)
2 Yukon Gold potatoes, peeled
50 g unsalted butter
30 mL extra-virgin olive oil
150 mL hot water
salt

MUJADDARA (RICE AND LENTILS WITH FRIED ONIONS) (page 128)

Serves 6–8

200 g French lentils (you can also use brown lentils)
200 g basmati rice, rinsed in cold water at least 5 times, until the water starts to run clear
30 g unsalted butter, divided
50 mL extra-virgin olive oil
1 bay leaf
2 large yellow onions, sliced into ½-cm half-moons
salt and freshly ground black pepper
2 sliced avocados, for serving
Tahini Dressing (page 33)

GREEK *FAVA* (YELLOW LENTILS WITH LEMON AND OLIVE OIL) (page 131)

Serves 6–8

500 g yellow lentils, rinsed very well (you can also use yellow split peas)
1 yellow onion, peeled and left whole
2 bay leaves
extra-virgin olive oil
fresh lemon juice
salt and freshly ground black pepper
½ red onion, thinly sliced or finely chopped (optional)
salt-packed capers (optional)

FALAFEL PARTY (page 132)

Serves 6–8, about 16 balls

500 g dried chickpeas, soaked overnight in plenty of water
1 small yellow onion, roughly chopped
2 garlic cloves
1 large handful of fresh flat-leaf parsley, roughly chopped (stems included)
1 large handful of fresh cilantro, roughly chopped (stems included)
1 handful of fresh mint, leaves only
5 g ground cumin
5 g ground coriander
2 g cayenne pepper
15 g all-purpose flour
salt and freshly ground black pepper
frying oil (safflower, canola, and vegetable oil all work well)

FISH

"GRILLED" WHOLE FISH, GREEK-STYLE (page 141)

Per person:

1 whole fish (Porgy, snapper, rainbow trout, and branzino are good choices. Ask your fishmonger to gut and scale the fish for you, keeping the head and tail intact. If the fish is really big, you can get one for two people to share.)
extra-virgin olive oil
salt and freshly ground black pepper
dried oregano
Latholemono (page 153)

SEARED TUNA (page 142)

Serves 4–6

50 g coarsely cracked black pepper
2 fresh tuna steaks about 2.5 cm thick (almost 500 g)
extra-virgin olive oil
salt

ROASTED SALMON (page 145)

Serves 8–10

1 side of salmon (around 1.5 kg)
extra-virgin olive oil
dried oregano
salt and freshly ground black pepper

Cooking temperature: 200 °C

FISH TACOS WITH LIME CREMA (page 146)

Serves 6–8

1 kg of your favorite fish (I like halibut, salmon, or sea bass)
juice of 1 lime
8 g ground cumin
3 g dried oregano
1 g cayenne pepper
2 g ground turmeric
extra-virgin olive oil
salt and freshly ground black pepper

Lime Crema:
200 g sour cream
zest and juice of 1 lime
extra-virgin olive oil
salt and freshly ground black pepper

Cooking temperature: 220 °C

WILD STRIPED BASS IN PARCHMENT WITH SWISS CHARD (page 148)

Serves 4

4 large leaves Swiss chard, any variety
1 whole lemon
500 g sea bass, halibut, or any white, fleshy fish, cut into 4 pieces
30 g cold unsalted butter
4 sprigs of fresh thyme
4 sheets parchment paper, each approximately 30 cm long
extra-virgin olive oil
salt and freshly ground black pepper

Cooking temperature: 200 °C

SALSAS AND OTHER FIXINGS

APPLE FENNEL SALSA (page 150)

1 Granny Smith apple, finely diced
1 fennel bulb, finely diced
juice of 2 limes
1 jalapeño, minced (remove the seeds for less heat)
1 large handful of fresh cilantro, finely chopped
2 scallions, thinly chopped, white and light-green parts only
salt and freshly ground black pepper

GRAPE SALSA WITH MINT (page 150)

200 g seedless red or purple grapes, each sliced into quarters
1 jalapeño, minced (use less for less heat)
juice of 1 lime
1 handful of fresh cilantro, chopped
1 handful of fresh mint, chopped
salt and freshly ground black pepper

AVOCADO SALSA (page 152)

2 ripe avocados, diced or thinly sliced
1 handful of fresh cilantro, leaves picked off and left whole
1 jalapeño, thinly sliced
extra-virgin olive oil
juice of 2 limes or 1 lemon
salt and freshly ground black pepper

MANGO SALSA (page 152)

3 mangoes, peeled and diced
juice of 2 limes
1 jalapeño, minced or grated on a Microplane
1 large handful of fresh cilantro, chopped
salt and freshly ground black pepper

RADISH, WATERCRESS, AND BASIL SALAD (page 153)

1 bunch of radishes, washed and trimmed
1 large bunch of watercress (thick stems removed)
1 small handful of basil leaves, coarsely torn
extra-virgin olive oil
juice of 1 lemon
salt and freshly ground black pepper

LATHOLEMONO (OLIVE OIL AND LEMON DRESSING) (page 153)

80 mL extra-virgin olive oil
50 mL fresh lemon juice
a generous pinch of dried oregano
salt and freshly ground black pepper

QUICK LEMON AIOLI (page 154)

30 mL fresh lemon juice
zest of 1 lemon
60 g mayonnaise
30 mL extra-virgin olive oil
a pinch of salt and freshly ground black pepper

ALEX'S HOT SAUCE (page 154)

24 whole garlic cloves, peeled and divided
10 red chili peppers (the long, skinny kind), stems removed
50 g granulated sugar
40 g salt
90 mL rice wine vinegar
40 mL water
3 g ground cumin
15 mL fish sauce
2 mL sesame oil

MEAT

salt and freshly ground black pepper

SMOKY SPICED CHICKEN KEBABS (page 163)

Serves 4–6

1 kg boneless, skinless breasts or thigh
salt and freshly ground black pepper
6–10 metal skewers

Marinade:
juice of 2 lemons
10 g cumin, seeds or powder
5 g ground coriander
3 g ground turmeric
2 g smoked Spanish-style paprika
15 g Dijon mustard
2 garlic cloves, finely chopped
3 g dried oregano
50 mL extra-virgin olive oil

GREEK-STYLE SEARED SKIRT STEAK WITH LEMON AND OREGANO (page 158)

Serves 4

juice of 1 lemon
1 garlic clove, finely chopped
15 g Dijon mustard
3 g dried oregano
15 mL extra-virgin olive oil
500 g skirt steak
salt and freshly ground black pepper

SEARED DUCK BREAST WITH ROASTED GRAPES AND SOUR CREAM MUSTARD (page 160)

Serves 2

1 Moulard duck breast
salt and freshly ground black pepper

Cooking temperature: 200 °C

Roasted Purple Grapes:
1–2 bunches of seedless purple grapes, left on the vine
extra-virgin olive oil
salt and freshly ground black pepper

Cooking temperature: 200 °C

Sour Cream Mustard:
15 g Dijon mustard
50 g sour cream
15 mL fresh lemon juice

KOKKINISTO (BRAISED BEEF WITH TOMATOES, CINNAMON, AND CLOVES) (page 164)

Serves 4–6

1 kg beef stew meat, cubed
50 mL red wine
2 yellow onions, finely chopped
2 bay leaves
1 cinnamon stick
3 whole cloves
400 g diced or crushed tomatoes
1 fresh tomato, chopped (optional)
salt and freshly ground black pepper
1 handful of fresh dill, chopped
Parmesan, for serving
pasta or orzo, for serving

PERSIAN CHICKEN STEW (page 166)

Serves 6–8

1 chicken (1–1.5 kg) cut into 10 serving pieces, skin removed (I leave out the wings, but feel free to include them)
1 large yellow onion, finely chopped
extra-virgin olive oil
4 garlic cloves, minced
2 bay leaves
1 cinnamon stick
3 g ground turmeric
3 g ground coriander
8 g ground cumin
250 g green beans, fresh or frozen, ends trimmed
400 g pureed tomatoes
salt and freshly ground black pepper

BRAISED SPICED LAMB WITH YOGURT AND WALNUTS (page 170)

Serves 6–8

Spiced Lamb:
1 kg lamb stew meat, cubed
50 g all-purpose flour
1 large yellow onion, finely chopped
4 garlic cloves, finely chopped
2 bay leaves
10 g ground cumin
3 g ground coriander
1 cinnamon stick
3 g hot red pepper flakes
2 medium carrots, peeled and sliced on the bias into ½-cm discs
2 dL dry red wine or chicken broth
400 g pureed tomatoes
extra-virgin olive oil
salt and freshly ground black pepper

Yogurt Sauce:
500 g Greek yogurt
15 mL fresh lemon juice
50 mL extra-virgin olive oil
salt and freshly ground black pepper

Garnishes:
100 g raw walnuts, toasted using Technique #1 and chopped
1 handful of fresh flat-leaf parsley, mint, or cilantro leaves, finely chopped

Cooking temperature: 200 °C

SWEET THINGS

PEARS WITH LEMON, CINNAMON, AND HONEY (page 179)

Serves 6–8

4 just ripe pears, your favorite type (Anjou is mine)
juice of 1 lemon
honey (preferably Greek thyme honey)
a sprinkle of cinnamon

GREEK YOGURT PANNA COTTA WITH MASTIC AND APRICOT COMPOTE (page 180)

Serves 8

Panna Cotta:
30 mL water
30 mL fresh lemon juice
10 g unflavored gelatin
550 g whole-milk Greek yogurt
400 mL heavy cream, divided
100 g granulated sugar
2 g ground mastic
vegetable oil, for greasing

Apricot Compote:
15 fresh apricots, halved with pits removed
30 g granulated sugar
15 mL water
10 mL fresh lemon juice
5 mL pure vanilla extract

MAPLE YOGURT WITH BERRY COMPOTE (page 182)

Serves 6

Maple Yogurt:
80 mL pure maple syrup
500 g whole-milk or 2% Greek yogurt

Berry Compote:
500 g strawberries, hulled and cut in half
150 g blueberries, blackberries, raspberries, or a mix
5 mL pure vanilla extract
10 mL fresh lemon juice
30 g granulated sugar

MILK CHOCOLATE PUDDING WITH VANILLA CREAM (page 185)

Serves 6

Chocolate Pudding:
30 g granulated sugar
15 g cornstarch
15 g unsweetened cocoa powder
1 g salt
350 mL whole milk
120 mL heavy cream
150 g fine-quality milk chocolate, broken into pieces
5 mL pure vanilla extract

Vanilla Cream:
250 mL heavy cream
15 g granulated sugar
1 vanilla bean

STRAWBERRY RHUBARB CRUMBLE (page 186)

Serves 8

Fruit Filling:
1.5 kg fresh strawberries, hulled and cut in half
150 g fresh rhubarb, cut into ½-cm dice
50 g granulated sugar
15 mL fresh lemon juice
5 mL pure vanilla extract

Crumble:
200 g all-purpose flour
50 g granulated sugar
3 g salt
zest of 1 orange
a pinch of ground nutmeg
140 g unsalted butter, chilled and cut into small cubes
170 g old-fashioned oats
150 g raw pecans, coarsely chopped
vanilla ice cream or whipped cream, for serving

Cooking temperature: 180 °C

PLUM AND GREEK YOGURT TIRAMISU (page 189)

Serves 8–10

Plum Compote:
1.5 kg plums, quartered and pitted
100 g granulated sugar
15 mL balsamic vinegar
1 cinnamon stick

Cream Base:
300 g mascarpone
250 g 2% Greek yogurt
60 mL heavy cream
50 g granulated sugar
5 mL pure vanilla extract
2 g ground cinnamon
200 g package Italian lady fingers

OLIVE OIL CAKE (page 191)

Serves 10–12

3 large eggs
350 mL extra-virgin olive oil
250 g granulated sugar, plus 10 g to sprinkle on top
300 mL milk
60 mL cognac (optional)
60 mL fresh orange juice
zest of 1 orange
250 g all-purpose flour
2.5 g baking soda
2.5 g baking powder
6 g ground cinnamon
2 g ground cloves
5 g salt

Cooking temperature: 180 °C

BANANA BREAD WITH WALNUTS AND DARK CHOCOLATE (page 192)

Makes one loaf

200 g all-purpose flour
5 g baking soda
5 g baking powder
1.5 g salt
100 g granulated or brown sugar
120 g unsalted butter, at room temperature
3 large overripe bananas, peeled
2 large eggs
5 mL pure vanilla extract
15 mL fresh lemon juice
50 g or more bittersweet chocolate, cut into small pieces
50 g raw walnuts, chopped

Cooking temperature: 180 °C

PISTACHIO ORANGE FLOWER COOKIES (page 194)

Makes about 24

100 g raw pistachios
200 g all-purpose flour
2.5 g baking powder
1.5 g salt
110 g unsalted butter, at room temperature
40 g confectioners' sugar, plus more for rolling
1 large egg yolk
15 mL brandy or cognac
5 mL pure vanilla extract
15 mL orange flower water

Cooking temperature: 180 °C

BAKLAVA (page 196)

Makes about 40 pieces

Baklava:
30 g granulated sugar
5 g ground cinnamon
4 g ground cloves
300 g raw walnuts
200 g raw almonds
220 g unsalted butter
500 g package phyllo, thawed (follow manufacturer's directions)

Honey Syrup:
350 g honey (preferably Greek thyme honey)
500 mL water
1 cinnamon stick
15 mL fresh lemon juice

Cooking temperature: 180 °C

Hope Atherton, *radish*, 2014

ACKNOWLEDGMENTS

THANK YOU,

Urs Fischer, from the bottom of my heart, for your support, for your total belief in my cooking, and for thinking I make the best turkey at Thanksgiving, even though you don't really like turkey. Working with you on this book has been a dream come true, and thanking you will never seem like enough.

Gavin Brown, for never forgetting to toast me at every single dinner I've cooked since 2006. Thank you for making the GBE kitchen a second home.

Corinna Durland, for letting me make bouillabaisse instead of curry, and Lisa Ivorian-Jones, for being my Kevin Bacon.

Elizabeth Peyton, for telling me that what we are best at comes to us easily.

Priya Bhatnagar, for being the most amazing editor a girl could ask for. Thank you for encouraging me to use my own voice and for honestly telling me when I couldn't share your desk. You were supportive throughout this entire project and your knowledge of grammar will never cease to amaze me. (A "dangler"!?)

Domie Clausen, for dominating the layout with awesomeness.
Jaz Harold, for jazifying those photographs and making me look good.

Katherine Krause, for editing, and helping to bring the concept of the book to light. Mira Evnine, for tirelessly testing recipes, conversions, and letting me lay on your couch. Dervla Kelly, for your keen eye. Suzanne Fass, for the excellent index. Kristina Williamson, for your effort and patience.

To the incredibly talented artists—Hope Atherton, Darren Bader, Matthew Barney, Alex Eagleton, Urs Fischer, Cassandra MacLeod, Elizabeth Peyton, Rob Pruitt and all at his studio, Peter Regli, Josh Smith, Spencer Sweeney, and Philippos Theodorides—thank you for contributing your drawings to this book.

To my parents, James and Evgenia Stone, for your undying support of all my creative endeavors since I was a little girl and for being my biggest fans, always. I am a very lucky daughter.

Yiayia mou, your tiropita shop would make millions. Thank you for all that you have taught me. Maxeen Stone, for frozen cool whip and glitzy jewelry, I miss you.

Miriam Stone for encouraging me to write, Margarita Inez for all those Sklavenitis trips and your translations. Patricia Stone, my health and product guru. Marlon Aitcheson, for helping me get started.

To my wonderful and supportive friends, Amy Dehuff, Kirsten Deirup, Erika Gable, Jarrett Gregory, Rachel Katwan, Daphne Lopez, Cassandra MacLeod, Randi Mates, Aly Mostel, and Julie Miller.

To everyone at GBE, throughout the years, especially Scarlett Connolly—the backbone of gallery dinners—and Daniel Baez.

To the rest of the Mr. Keet studio crew, past and present: Philipp Bachmann, Frankie Brun, Serena Chang, Ted Christensen, Carmen D'Apollonio, Jaime Gecker, Aric Grauke, Abby Haywood, Diana Ho, Karen Jordan, Angela Kunicky, Mats Nordman, Jonny Onetime, and Caleb Rogers—what would I do without you guys? Your yays when the bell dings and your total enthusiasm about this book coming to life mean the world to me. Thank you all.

Alex Eagleton, thank you for your constant support in every step of making this book. It wouldn't have been the same without your photos, your taste testing, and your sense of humor. You are my favorite person to cook with and my favorite person in general.

CREDITS

PHOTOGRAPHY CREDITS

All photography by Mina Stone except for the following:
Alex Eagleton: 11, 58, 59, 112, 135, 136, 173, back endpaper
Daniel Egneus: back cover
Urs Fischer: front endpaper, 45, 62, 83
Cassandra MacLeod: 169

ARTWORK CREDITS

Page 3:
Cassandra MacLeod, *Purrr-a Vida*, 2014
Ink and Aquarelle
8 x 10 inches
Courtesy of the artist

Page 28:
Josh Smith, 2015
Pencil on paper
Courtesy of the artist

Page 63:
Elizabeth Peyton and Matthew Barney, *The Hosts*, 2014
Etching in black ink on Magnani Pescia Soft White Paper
11¾ x 7¾ inches
Courtesy of the artists and Two Palms, New York

Page 85:
Rob Pruitt, *Studio Stew*, 2014
Sharpie markers on paper
Drawers include Rob Pruitt, Daniel Oh, Tatiana Westin-McCaw, Kevin Stahl, Aliyana Gewirtzman, Keegan Monaghan, Kathryn Kerr, and Sophy Naess
Courtesy of the artists

Page 118:
Alex Eagleton, *Sometimes Always*, 2014
Ink on paper towel
Courtesy of the artist

Page 137:
Urs Fischer, *Merpig*, 2014
Courtesy of the artist

Page 175:
Peter Regli, *thank you mina stone*, 2014
Chinese ink on paper
9 x 12 inches
Courtesy of the artist

Pages 198–199:
Spencer Sweeney, *Dinner*, 2014
Pencil on paper and collage
8½ x 11 inches
Courtesy of the artist

Page 217:
Hope Atherton, *radish*, 2014
Ink on paper
Courtesy of the artist

Page 220:
Darren Bader, *518 days a year*, 2014
Courtesy of the artist

Page 227:
Philippos Theodorides, *Stray Cat*, 2014
Ink on paper
Courtesy of the artist

518 DAYS A YEAR

INDEX

L

M

N

O

P

T

Philippos Theodorides, *Stray Cat*, 2014

I DON'T LIKE
FASOLAKI

TDA
ATLIS
LIFO-512